Steel Wheels and Rubber Tyres

Volume One

Transport around Oldham in the 1930s
Locomotives at Gorton in the 1940s
Leeds Trams in the 1950s

by
Geoffrey Hilditch
OBE, Ch Engr, FI Mech E, FILT, FCIT, MIRTE

THE OAKWOOD PRESS

British Library Cataloguing in Publication Data
A Record for this book is available from the British Library
ISBN 0 85361 614 0

Typeset by Oakwood Graphics.
Repro by Ford Graphics, Ringwood, Hants.
Printed by Cambrian Printers, Aberystwyth, Ceredigion.

Photographs

Over the years I have managed to acquire a considerable number of photographs and many of these are included where they are germain to the story in this publication. In many instances I have no knowledge as to who actually took them, and so they must remain unnamed, but I do pay full tribute to their excellent and much appreciated efforts. Sadly some old friends who were active in the field such as Bob Parr, Bob Mack, and W.A. Camwell are no longer with us, but I look back with pleasure on the conversations that we had, and the way in which they were prepared to open their files to me, whenever I made a request.

Finally despite the size of my collection I found that I was short of several pertinent pictures and here I am more than obliged to David Wayman, Roy Marshall and Brian Render (like me a former member of the staff of the Leeds drawing office), old friends who took trouble to search out those that I was wanting.

Front cover, top: Ex-GCR 'C13' class 4-4-2T No. 67438 looking immaculate in BR lined black livery as it propels its ex-GCR two-coach push-and-pull set at Hyde Junction in 1952. *W. Oliver/Colour-Rail*

Front cover, bottom: Leeds single-deck tram No. 601 at Hunslet terminus in May 1955. *W.E. Robertson/Colour-Rail*

Rear cover, top: In 1928 Oldham acquired its last Huddersfield-built Karrier chassis. No. 43 BU 5550 was the first of six fitted with English Electric 66-seat bodies and here stands when brand new at the Alexandra Park Gates. It lasted until 1933. Note the ornamental drinking fountain moved from the Market Place a year or two earlier. I included this picture to show how bus design had developed in just 10 years when petrol engines were out and diesel engines in giving from 5 mpg to 10 mpg and improved performance.

Rear cover, bottom: Fowler 2-6-2T No. 40059 leaves Lees with the Delph Donkey in April 1954. The train consists of an Oerlikon electric coach converted for push-and-pull operation and an ex-London & North Western Railway motor trailer. Note the snow, a very common feature in winter in my younger days. *Jim Davenport/Colour-Rail*

Published by The Oakwood Press (Usk), P.O. Box 13, Usk, Mon., NP15 1YS.
E-mail: oakwood-press@dial.pipex.com
Website: www.oakwood-press.dial.pipex.com

Contents

The author standing at the controls of a Newcastle tram. This photograph was taken outside Central station while visiting Newcastle in June 1946. Car No. 102 was a member of the 89-110 series built by Newcastle in 1903 as very large bogie open-toppers. Several were rebuilt over the years but No. 102 remained largely in original condition. As such it was acquired for preservation on its withdrawal and so continues in existence.

Foreword

Very few road passenger transport professionals, and especially those involved in the now almost vanished municipal sector, have ever taken the trouble to write down for publication a record of their activities which would include an outline of the engineering, operation and financial/administrative problems that came their daily way, and what a story so many of them could have told.

Just what must it have been like to set up and then run a brand new *circa* 1900s electric tramway system or to cope later with the vagaries of those temperamental 1920s buses, or in the 1930s to start to abandon tramcars for motor or trolley buses or to engage in the initial and quite unprecedented traffic court battles?

Consequently here is my attempt to provide present day passenger transport enthusiasts with just a flavour of what it was like to be so involved from the middle of the last century through the next few decades, when almost non-stop change was the name of the name.

Before one reached the dizzy heights of finding the legend 'General Manager' affixed to your office door one had to obtain a suitable start in the industry and thereafter try to make progress as opportunity allowed.

If anything, obtaining that first start could be far from easy as it certainly was in my case as none of my local municipal or company concerns were at all interested in providing me with my first ever job, indeed some did not deign to answer my requests even when an SAE was included.

Here then is the story of how one interested but uninformed schoolboy tried to attain his early and overriding ambition to see his name in gold leaf on the side, preferably of a municipal tramcar, against those almost magic words 'General Manager', when a certain uncle was certainly a catalyst. Why I was first bitten with the transport bug one Saturday night in Stockport I know not, but now finally retired at 77 can only say 'Thank goodness that I was'.

Where it all began. I took this photograph of Disley station in May 1966 when it was quite unchanged from my childhood days.

Chapter One

In the Beginning

I was born in the now long gone 1920s in the village of Disley, our house, Ashlea, in Red House Lane being off the main Stockport to Buxton road which ran through the village and which in those days saw relatively few cars or commercial vehicles passing up and down.

My parents both came from large families, father being the eldest of 10 children, and mother the eldest of nine, and as a result they were in no doubt that one, or at the most, two children were quite enough, but as it transpired I never did come to have either a brother or a sister. Father, born in 1891, was a native of Denshaw which is still little more than a hamlet, some six miles from Oldham on the main Halifax road. He started work in the Calico Print Works there as a part timer at the age of 12, going full time on his 13th birthday, but around 1913 as a young man moved to the similar establishment in Newton-le-Willows where he met mother. I have little doubt that had it not been for the outbreak of World War I they would have been married at least eight years before that happy event occurred, in 1922.

As it was, father volunteered for the forces when he and his friend Brandon, who was later to be killed by his side during the Battle of the Somme, walked all the way from Denshaw to Halifax, and there enlisted in the West Yorkshire Regiment. This process took place in the former Highroad Well tram shed. As he was wont to say in later years, a medical examination there in mid-winter when snow was on the ground was a stimulating experience. The walk home after all this must have been another.

Now, though, in 1926 he was working at the Calico Printers Association (CPA) factory at Strines so twice a day walked to and from it making use of the tow path of the Peak Forest canal, which was still well used in this period.

From my point of view, Red House lane was well situated. Go up it a few yards and on the main road ran the buses of the North Western Road Car Company, these being then a fairly recent innovation and much appreciated by the local residents in consequence.

Go down the lane, and there was the bridge carrying the former London and North Western Railway's (LNWR) Stockport to Buxton line, whilst a little further down was the bridge where the Midland Railway's expensive 'cut off' from Heaton Mersey to Chinley crossed. This also at this time was of quite recent vintage, not having been opened to traffic until 1st July, 1902. It was not very long before the parents came to realise that the best way to quieten a fractious child was to take him to see the trains, and whilst there were these two local possibilities, an even better way was to walk through the village to the former LNWR station and there sit in comfort whilst son happily awaited developments.

Most Saturdays we went to Stockport for shopping or entertainment purposes, sometimes by train, sometimes by bus, and here I have strong memories of being on what was then known as Edgeley station and seeing

Early North Western Tilling Stevens had removable canvas roofs but by 1928 a permanent form had been adopted. B10 fleet number 227 (DB 5127) was one of 66 vehicles purchased that year with orthodox transmission. This one had a Brush 36-seat body and an unladen weight of 4-12-1.

The eight Oldham AEC buses were impressive vehicles in their time, being the fleet's first double-deckers. Eight in number dating from 1926, fleet Nos. 10-17. Here No. 12 poses at the bodybuilder's (Charles Roe) works when new. Pneumatic tyres were fitted in 1928.

carriages still painted in the colours of the old LNWR. Bus trips involved catching our homewards-bound North Western chariot in Mersey Square, a location then rather different from what it is today. It was there one evening after lighting up time that I saw my first 'Green Linnet', or in other words a tramcar of the erstwhile Stalybridge, Hyde, Mossley and Duckinfield Joint Board (SHMD), which for some obscure reason made a big impression. According to my parents I cried bitterly for a 'scody' and they could not make out just what it was that I wanted, but I have no doubts that I desired to be taken for a ride on this green stranger that looked to be so different from the red Stockport and Manchester trams seen in the centre of Stockport, or the North Western buses that sported the same basic colour. Sad to say, I did not get my ride on an SHMD tram until several more years had passed.

I did, though, have a ride on our furniture lorry, as a little while later when 2½-years old we moved to a house in Strines, which was much more convenient for father, but not so convenient in other respects, as lighting was by oil lamps, no fire in the living room meant no hot water, and a small brick building in the garden house provided the sanitary facilities.

More North Western buses passed right in front of our house (Hilly View) and again these were invariably based on Tilling Stevens chassis with either Tilling or Brush single-deck bodies. These worked from Stockport (or later Manchester) to Hayfield via Marple, Strines and New Mills but this was a period when hiking was a popular summer pastime and so the Hayfield service tended to come under pressure. When this occurred open-topped double-decked Tilling Stevens 51-seaters would appear. North Western then had 24 of these 1925 vintage open-topped machines that ran on solid tyres, and invariably made me feel queasy whenever I travelled on one. But then in 1929 a series of Leyland-bodied Leyland 'Tiger' single-deckers were taken into stock. Fifteen in number, I recall being impressed on my first trips on them by the 'jelly mould' clear glass lamp shades that housed the interior light bulbs, and their obviously improved performance over their Tilling predecessors.

Another stranger to appear one fine morning was a prototype Crossley double-decker that obligingly suffered from some technical difficulty hard by our garden gate, giving one small boy the chance to give it a thorough looking over. But eventually mobility was restored and it left in a cloud of exhaust smoke in the Stockport direction.

Smoke was also apparent across the valley from our home as trains passed along the Midland and Great Central Joint line and this we used very frequently, as mother did most of her shopping in New Mills. Although it was much further to walk to Strines station, than to catch a bus almost at the door, trains formed our invariable conveyances, so I presume there was a fare advantage.

Most trains that we caught were of Great Central Railway (GCR) origin being made up of gas lit six-wheeled coaches, and hauled by an ex-GCR 2-4-2 tank locomotive based at Gorton, but of that place then I knew not. Occasionally a London, Midland & Scottish Railway (LMS) train travelling to Chinley or beyond was caught instead, and certainly the coaches we then travelled in were much superior to those in the London & North Eastern Railway's (LNER) varnished teak livery. But for some reason that I could not define I much

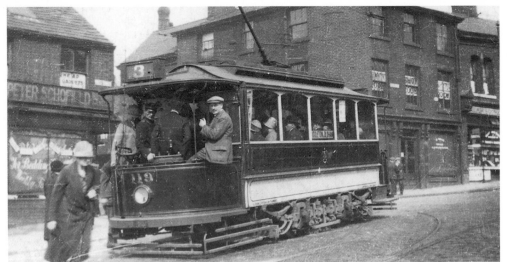

Close to home, car No. 119 has just passed our old shop as it climbs up West Street towards its Market Place terminus. The car and its route from Middleton via Chadderton were acquired from the Middleton Electric Traction Co. in August 1925. Oldham initially laid several unnecessary junctions and here was one - a pair of tracks leading left into Rochdale Road. Disconnected when lines were laid in Upper West Street in 1912, the curves and the corresponding right-hand double-track curves into San Domingo Street survived until all tracks were lifted after closure of the Middleton/Mills Hill Bridge service in June 1935. The overhead had, however, to be kept *in situ* until 1939 to feed power to the Featherstall Road section (Route 8).

A 'Green Linnet'. My old friend W.A. Camwell took this photograph of of a SHMD car in Acres Lane, Dukinfield on 18th September, 1937 when tramway operation in this area was on very much a part time basis. This was one car I could not have seen that night in Stockport around 1928/1929 as it would not have passed safely under the low Woodley railway bridge which crossed the Hyde to Stockport and Edgeley tramway route. The side route board is for the Mottram service but by the above date that was no more.

preferred LNER offerings even though mother often grumbled about how hard it was to turn the door handles on the six-wheelers. Things, though, were happening at Strines, for the new print works was in the course of construction, and a large number of roof girders were being received in the goods yard where they were unloaded by the yard crane. One day when this work was in progress a girder swung too far as a train was passing with the result that the locomotive lost its funnel in the ensuing encounter and I was rather pleased that it was an LMS rather than an LNER engine that had suffered. Why do such prejudices form so early in life?

I was not though so prejudiced against the next innovation of the North Western company as 1931 saw the arrival of modernity in the shape of six all-Leyland double-deckers of the low bridge design. Needless to say the upper saloon front seat was my favourite but my trips on them were to be all too few, as hardly had they appeared than we were on the move. My father, after suffering a wage reduction at Strines as a result of the depression and the closure of so many CPA factories, had been lucky in obtaining a more lucrative situation only two miles or so from his birth place of Denshaw. And so to the village of Delph we moved in the late summer of 1931, where I met two disappointing problems. Firstly none of my school friends would believe my assertions that North Western *did* have modern double-deckers, for the Tillings had previously been seen in the area, and were for obvious reasons well remembered, and secondly no LNER trains were to be seen, so I had to exist on what the LMS could offer, and I was not impressed.

I must here mention something that did intrigue me. At this time Union Road in New Mills boasted a toy shop and in the window for quite a long period stood a large tin plate model of a Sentinel steam wagon, finished in a buff colour, with brown lining. The cab had a brass boiler with its chimney sprouting through the cab roof, but this wonderful toy was not steam-powered but clockwork. Beneath the boiler was a representation of the ash pan, and this could be illuminated when, thanks to a dry battery, an internal bulb and a celluloid lining, it would glow red. There was a tipping body, and for a small boy it really was a fascinating toy. Having mother take me to look at this treasure week after week finally registered, and on my birthday which occurred shortly before we left Strines that Sentinel became mine.

I often wondered in later days which firm made it, and how much my father paid for it, for he was then on a quite small wage, and it was obviously not cheap to buy. Despite being a toy it looked very authentic, and in all the days since I have never seen another one like it.

I did often meet a real steam wagon once we had arrived in Delph, this being a Foden 'Overtype'. Painted dark blue it was owned by Edwin Butterworth and Company, the proprietors of the Denshaw Print Works where my father had been employed, and was used mainly to carry coal from the Delph station coal drops to Denshaw Vale. It was driven by a Mr Kershaw who was closely related to our next door neighbour, and so from time to time I was allowed on the footplate. In previous years, however, the print works steamer had been used for passenger work, and my aunts could tell hilarious tales of how Sunday school outings had seen them board the flat behind the cab, and there in their

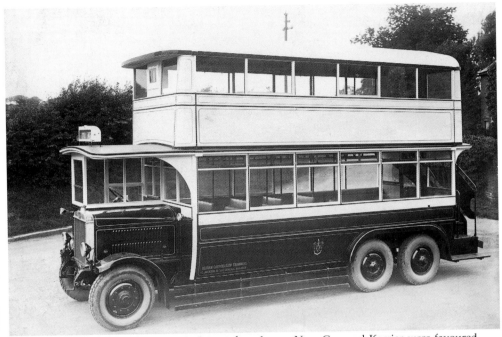

No more AEC buses ever came to be purchased new. Now Guy and Karrier were favoured, usually of the three-axle variety. The Guys, Nos. 33 and 34, arrived in 1927. These were the last vehicles to have open staircase bodies, the C.H. Roe concern was the builder. They went into service on 26th September.

Oldham purchased two Karrier single-deckers with 39-seat Short bodies in 1927, Nos. 28 and 29, and six more, Nos. 37 to 42, with Hall Lewis 33-seat bodies in 1928. They looked potent, and were in more way than one, despite a legal speed limit of 12 mph. Here is one of the last six again when brand new.

The Ripponden & District concern gave up its stage carriage services in 1936 when North Western and Yorkshire Woollen took over its Bradford-Halifax-Manchester workings. The Halifax Joint Committee acquired the local routes together with some of its speedy vehicles. Here is a Leyland 'Tiger' now painted in Halifax colours.

No. 54 was one of eight Guy FCX double-deck vehicles with English Electric 70-seat bodies, Nos. 49 to 56. New in 1928 they formed Oldham's last batch of three-axled buses. In November 1928 Mr Jackson, the General Manager, left to take up a similar post at Plymouth to be replaced by J.F. Richards, the rolling stock superintendent, who had different ideas.

summer dresses sit on forms taken from the school. If your seat was hard by the cab backboard all might be well, but be nearer the rear, and a pristine white dress was soon covered in spots of soot as was the rest of your person.

Before the print works took to steam wagons, horses were used and when the wagon full of printed cloth left for Manchester trace horses were used to pull the load up to Grains Bar, from where it was downhill all the way. The carter took with him a couple of homing pigeons, and when coming back the following day with the grey cloth for next week's printing released the birds around Failsworth. Their return to Denshaw was closely watched, and then the trace horses set out to meet the load in Oldham and so provide extra power for the climb to Grains Bar. The staff also looked out for that wagon, for a full load of cloth meant a full week's work, and hence a full week's wage. A light load meant gloom all round, and still more gloom followed when in due course steam and a telephone replaced pigeons and Shire horses. The Foden, though, had a long life running until the works closed around 1939.

The original of this photograph which depicts an early Manchester Crossley is dated 11th March, 1930. It was a bus like this that developed a 'technical fault' by my Strines garden gate. Note the front offside lower deck emergency door. The side route board covers the famous No. 53 route - the first Manchester major tramway conversion.

Chapter Two

The Youthful Scene

I well remember our journey from Strines to Delph. We caught a bus to Stockport and a train from Edgeley to Oldham Clegg Street, then I had my first ride on the 'Delph Donkey' as it was known locally.

There was at this time quite a good train service between the two terminals worked on the push-and-pull principle, when four coaches, no two of which were ever alike, were powered by a Webb 0-6-2 ex-LNWR coal tank stationed at Lees Shed. All the trains were made up of corridor stock as the guard issued tickets or collected the same from passengers joining or leaving at the halts at Grasscroft, Moorgate for Uppermill and Dobcross. Several of the more modern carriages had been lavatory fitted, but on these the toilet doors were sealed up so Delph line passengers had to do without convenience facilities. One regular set had a most unusual vehicle, in that although of the corridor compartment type, no doors were fitted to the compartments on the corridor side nor did it seem from a careful inspection had any ever been provided.

The weather though on this first trip was quite foggy, and whilst father tried to show me where the Saddleworth viaduct was, all I could see of it was the first 50 yards or so vanishing into the murk. It was not much better as we walked from the station to our new house, which, despite being quite new and having both gas lighting and a bathroom, was not in an exactly popular location as the end wall lay parallel to the boundary of a graveyard. But in our stay there we never saw any ghosties or heard things that went bump in the night.

At the time of our arrival Delph station boasted a signal box, but this alas then burned down and was replaced by a ground frame, but if there was a reduction here in facilities a new one about half a mile down the line soon followed in the shape of Measurements Halt. This consisted of a short platform and two lamp posts, with a like number of oil lamps. It gained its odd name from the nearby Measurements factory built by Hirst Brothers to make clocks, but then turned over to the production of electric meters. For at this very time the SHMD organisation was planting overhead line poles all over Saddleworth and, miracle of miracles, Delph was about to be supplied and our own house was in line for conversion too.

The village also boasted four bus services, the North Western Road Car Co. being much in evidence and working, usually with Tilling Stevens machines, services from Delph to Mossley (Brookbottom) and from an odd terminal at Friezeland Church though Uppermill, Delph and Denshaw to Newhey, which was not very frequent even in those pre-popular motoring days. These ran into, or through, the centre of the village but the other two, either from Gatley or Manchester to Delph, one way via Scouthead, or via Lees, on an hourly frequency each way, only served the station. To these were added supplementary routes again operating both ways, but starting from Greaves Street, Oldham this being hard by the then Union Street main post office. All these circular services circum-navigated the Delph station premises, and were so timed as to give equal half-hour frequencies from that point to Oldham in both directions. These semi-

The modern look. By the date of our move to Delph in 1931 North Western Tilling Stevens of the 516-577 series were sporting Brush bodies with sloping windscreens and deeper roofs. Seating capacity was 33. After this same year 12 more Tillings only this time with Tilling bodies were to be purchased, these appearing in 1932. Note the horn mounted under the canopy.

Delph station. The signal box stood a few yards from the end of the platform ramp. Bailey Mill to the left had its own private siding. For a few years (from 1887) tracks ran out of the far end of the station yard and then up Huddersfield Road (passed our third Delph house) to gain the so called 'Tram Road'. This was during the period when Oldham's Castleshaw reservoirs were being built. Two miles in all, it is hard to imagine that railway tracks were actually ever laid in Huddersfield Road and then on the still existing wide verge upwards from today's cricket field.

OLDHAM, GREENFIELD, AND DELPH BRANCHES.

Week Days.

	Oldham {Clegg St. dep / G. Road
Lees	
Grotton & Springhead	
Grasscroft	
Greenfield arr / dep	
Moorgate	
Dobcross	
Measurements	
Delph arr	

Week Days—continued.

Oldham {Clegg St. dep / G. Road	
Lees	
Grotton & Springhead	
Grasscroft	
Greenfield arr / dep	
Moorgate	
Dobcross	
Measurements	
Delph arr	

Week Days—continued.

Sundays.

Your Train to London is "The Comet."
5.45 p.m. from MANCHESTER (London Road), arriving Euston at 9.0 p.m.

Week Days.

Delph dep	
Measurements	
Dobcross	
Moorgate	
Greenfield arr / dep	
Grasscroft	
Grotton & Springhead	
Lees	
Oldham {G. Road arr / Clegg St.	

Week Days—continued.

Week Days—continued.

Sundays.

A—One class only.   B—One class only except on Saturdays.   SX—Saturdays excepted.

It's QUICKER BY RAIL!

Timetable for the 'Delph Donkey', from 26th September, 1938 until further notice.

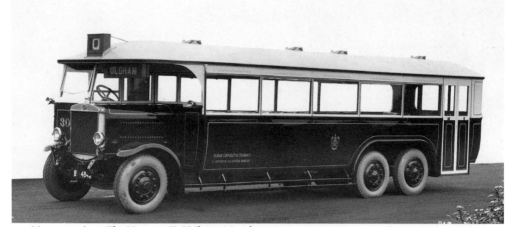

Not so modern. The Uppermill-Oldham-Manchester routes in 1931 were still extended to Gatley and saw thereon Oldham's three Guy/Roe 39-seat single-deckers Nos. 30 to 32 of 1927. I have vivid memories of sitting on a wall at Scouthead after one of the trio had found the climb from Waterhead up Austerland's rather too much for it and so came to an abrupt halt in a cloud of steam.

In 1931 Oldham purchased four Leyland 'Tiger'/Roe 31-seaters and five more followed in 1932, Nos. 59 to 67. All had petrol engines and they were far more reliable than the Guys or Karriers they came for the next few years to dominate the express services. I last rode on one from Oldham to Delph about 1946 but wondered if we too would ever make it as by the top of Austerland's we had a 'boil up' of steam locomotive proportions. During the war they were kept fully employed on service C, Star Inn to Middleton Junction. David Wayman kindly provided this illustration.

circular innovations were worked jointly with Manchester and Oldham Corporations, the Gatley routes being one of Henry Mattison's long distance innovations. They were sadly not destined to have a long life as the railway companies objected before the newly instituted Traffic Commissioners as soon as they could, so the Gatley service was cut back to Manchester (Lower Mosley Street) and then later still to the new Parker Street (Piccadilly) bus station. They finally ended up in my time in the area at Stevensons Square thanks to the Manchester blitz so these reductions did not exactly improve passenger convenience.

Henry Mattison had become General Manager of Manchester's Transport in 1922 and oddly enough lived at the time of my birth also in Disley in a house that was not all that far from ours. A strong supporter of tramway development, he nevertheless quickly realised how the development of the motor bus together with the competitive situation of the 1920s threatened the viability of municipal operations. Fighting fire with fire he sponsored a whole series of jointly worked express bus services into and across Manchester, the Uppermill, Oldham, Manchester Gatley service being just one of these, that numbered finally almost 30. Sadly Mr Mattison died whilst on holiday in Salcombe, Devon on 1st September, 1928 and his eventual successor, Mr R. Stuart Pilcher, had a very different philosophy, which had little time for tramcars.

Manchester at the time of our arrival in Delph used various Crossley or Leyland single-deckers on its routes, whilst Oldham provided various members of its Guy or Karrier three-axled saloons.

The Oldham fleet was then 58 strong of Leyland, AEC and Karrier or Guy manufacture, but changes were in the air. The three-axled machines were purchased during the regime of Captain Clement Jackson, who was the General Manager from 1925 to 1929 when he departed for the balmier climes of Plymouth, to be replaced by the then head of the engineering department John F. Richards.

As it happened none of these machines were strangers to me, as we had often visited Denshaw in previous years, from Disley or Strines, when the trip usually involved taking a train to what was then London Road station, walking down its sloping approach, and turning right at the foot to gain the yard of the Rochdale Canal Company. Here various 'pirate' operators rented terminal space, including the Ripponden & District concern whose smart fleet of blue Leyland and AEC single-deckers ran through Oldham, Denshaw and Sowerby Bridge to Halifax, whilst a later but again short-lived extension took the buses to their ultimate terminus at Bradford. This was a service that was noted for speed and reliability, something that was perhaps helped by the route taken out of Manchester, for this ran via Bradford* and Briscoe Lane until the main road was gained at Newton Heath. Incidentally Oldham buses had also been in a blue livery until Mr Richards changed the colour scheme to incorporate the distinctive reddish brown of the tramcars, but if the shade of blue had then been similar to that of the Ripponden concern performance was certainly not.

Sometimes my parents elected to do some shopping in Oldham, so we would use the Gatley service to the Market Place there, and later take the tram to Grains Bar, and then walk down the hill to Old Tame. This continued until late in 1928 when the trams were replaced by buses which ran through to Denshaw

* Bradford is a suburb of Manchester and not the Yorkshire city of the same name.

My first footplate rides were on LMS engines. My best friend's father was the maintenance supremo at Bailey Mill, Delph, whose chiefs never seemed to object to two small boys watching the horizontal tandem compound steam engine *Diamond Queen* at work, or spending time in the boilerhouse. Coal came in via a private siding off the regular morning goods when in the school holidays we would be invited to join the crew of the inevitable Aspinall 0-6-0 locomotive which left for Oldham at noon. Here is a typical member of the class engaged in shunting, not at Delph but at West Vale, Halifax on the rump of the former Stainland branch.

The original 'Tigers' were displaced on the express services in 1933 by nine more Roe-bodied buses this time with oil engines, Nos. 21 to 29. Then in 1934 came three fully-fronted examples, Nos. 18, 19 and 20, which struck a new note. The side destination was of glass with a red background built into the body and illuminated from within which made them route-bound. No. 18 ran on the 13 service, No. 19 on the No. 2 Manchester-Newhey, and No. 20 on Manchester-Greenfield. In 1936/37 No. 18 took me almost daily from Delph after lunch to my Uppermill school gates on some occasions with Uncle George at the wheel. The side glass destinations were painted out never to re-appear when the war began and with a frequency cut from hourly to two-hourly double-deckers entirely replaced No. 18.

Junction, and initially the open staircase AEC double-deckers were used. These, needless to say, had at that time solid tyres, plus a very narrow cab, which boasted an incredibly small windscreen, but in no time at all the Guys and Karriers also began to appear. The odd thing here was that the trams were allegedly removed due to the condition of the tracks in Ripponden road, but these same tracks continued in use as far as Watersheddings for some years - I guess until around 1934 - to provide a tram service to and from the Rugby ground there. Their presence standing on a long length of single track to a point just above Alva Road must have given quite a few motorists a nasty surprise as they speeded round the left-hand bend, as with the rest of the route quickly dismantled, who would expect to find a line of solid trams occupying the centre of what was then a none too wide highway?

Oldham was still, despite the closure also in 1928 of the Lees route, very much a tramway town, and a visit to the Market Place always gave me a good deal of pleasure. One could see at the top of West Street, then also very narrow, the odd looking single-deckers that ran to Middleton, or the double-deckers that, thanks to the existing low bridge, could not proceed beyond Mills Hill Bridge. Up and down George Street came the cars of the No. 12 Hollinwood via Hollins service, heading to town terminals, either in the High Street opposite Woolworths, or at Mumps, whilst Henshaw Street saw the No. 9 Shaw to Chadderton Road trams.

To gain Henshaw Street these had to use a facing crossover, run wrong road for a few yards, and then use a right-hand turnout to reach the single track in that thoroughfare, when off the start of this track ran a left-hand turnout to make connection with the lines in West Street. Through the midst of all this action ran the Waterhead to Hollinwood or Manchester trams, services number 1 and 20 respectively, together with the Hollinwood via Werneth short workings that used the High Street crossover (trailing) and displayed the service No. 11.

A goodly number of trams passed through this part of the town every hour, but Oldham never invested in many sets of automatic points so at the Market Place and again at Star Inn boys were employed to work the switches, whilst at other locations, e.g. Cross Street where the Shaw cars left the main line, the conductors or drivers had to do the necessary manually with a point iron.

In this period it seemed to me that the Manchester route was worked by the 1921 vestibuled balcony cars. Shaw to Chadderton Road had the 1924 enclosed trams (six in number) plus the similar Hollinwood works rebuilds Nos. 40, 49 and 54. Hollinwood via Hollins and the No. 7 service that connected Hathershaw with Summit, and ran via Star Inn, saw modernity in the shape of the 1926 Chamberlain cars Nos. 121-132, which were notable in having upholstered seats in the upper saloon, as did car No. 49 after its second rebuild and modernisation in 1932. A high percentage of the double-deck stock, plus the single-deckers at this stage, were open-fronted and these were to be seen everywhere at all times of the day, and soon began to look very antique once the semi-streamlined and very fast Manchester Pullmans, or Pilchers as we always knew them, took up their workings on the Manchester route.

The trams and buses fascinated me and by the age of about eight I wanted to be involved with them but then my interest came to be rather diluted by, of all things, smoking. Visiting Denshaw was not always a joyous occasion for a small

In 1934 Oldham purchased a Crossley Mancunian chassis and had it fitted with a Roe body to become No. 57. A second vehicle, No. 58, a Leyland with an English Electric body was also purchased. Five more similar Crossleys, Nos. 1-5, followed in 1935. These were not popular buses and came to appear by 1938/9 only on rush hour duties. After the war direct injection engines were fitted and they saw more all-day use until withdrawal in 1949/50.

In June 1935 tram scrapping began with the closure of routes 3 and 9. A large number of new buses were required including 26 Leyland 'TD3s' with Roe 54-seat bodies, Nos. 76-101, shown here lined up in the then Oldham Edge garage. This view has been included to show the type of buses usually found in the 'Blitz' period on the 'Brews'. Never on any single night did I find a Daimler or a Crossley included in the 40, or any of the older petrol-engined buses either.

Also included in the 1935 tramway conversion bus orders were three Leylands with Leyland metal-framed double-deck bodies, Nos. 102 to 104. This design with its outstanding front indicator boxes was not over successful and so was never as successful in Oldham as the teak-framed Roe product. A metal-framed MCW-bodied Leyland, No. 105, was also acquired at the same time, but no further pre-war bodies were purchased from the MCW organisation.

In the mid-1930s Tilling Stevens chassis were rebodied with this type of Eastern Counties body with very luxurious seating. They were very comfortable vehicles until several were fitted with perimeter seating during the war. Some, however, were never so treated having been withdrawn or sold by 1939.

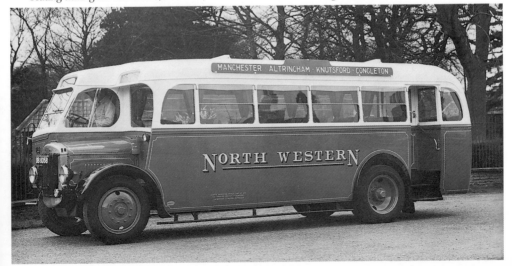

Unwanted and unloved Chamberlain car No. 125 stands on the Waterhead terminal stub shortly before abandonment. The 1939 repaint - which eliminated all lining out - has faded and the tram looks pretty decrepit. Even so reliability was still pretty good and I cannot recall ever seeing an Oldham tram that had failed in service and so was being towed back to Wallshaw depot during the war years. The same could not be said of certain Crossley buses that came onto the route (now No. 98 not 20) after the trams had passed into history.

The now demolished six-road shed at Lees, formerly an LNWR establishment, provided the motive power for local operations but 'Jubilees' and Pacifics did not figure on the roster. Here long time residents such as Fowler 0-8-0s, ex-L&Y 0-6-0s and Fowler push-and-pull fitted 2-6-2 tanks await their next call to duty. Here was a rather decrepit shed roof which was later repaired when the six roads were reduced to five. Lees Shed finally closed on Sunday 12th April, 1964. Delph and Greenfield passenger workings had ended earlier on Saturday 30th April, 1955.

boy. Grandma was kindly, but the house also was home to four of father's then unmarried sisters, who rather intimidated me, plus a still single brother who was an avid smoker. One day perhaps feeling a bit sorry for me, he gave me a cigarette coupon catalogue to look at , and something therein took my eye. If you could acquire just 260 BDV coupons you could become the possessor of a Bassett Lowke 4-4-0 tender locomotive . . . the tender came free, and for still more, track and coaches were on offer, whilst Kensitas also came to make similar offers. I exerted a certain amount of pressure, and in due course when various family members began to suffer from those ailments induced by smoking I began to feel a degree of remorse, but that was not to come for many years. What did come arrived on my 7th birthday, by which time we were living in our second Delph house, a house which had electricity and a very suitable unfurnished attic.

There was a green *Princess Elizabeth* locomotive and tender, two coaches and a goodly set of 2 ft radius curved rails plus several straights. The engine was painted green, and the coaches were lettered LNER so what price the LMS Delph donkey now? I had the best train set in the area, and those of my school compatriots who gave their allegiance to 'that other lot' were not amused, but then they never travelled through Guide Bridge. We did when we went back to visit friends living around our old haunts, and it was there that I saw a green LNER 'Director' class locomotive rather similar in appearance to my own 4-4-0 on an express carrying coach roofboards that read 'London Marylebone, Leicester, Nottingham, Sheffield, Manchester'. My interest in matters LNER deepened, and fortunately we began to travel through Guide Bridge quite often using the Delph train to Oldham Clegg Street, and then the LNER local from that point to Guide Bridge where we changed yet again onto a Romiley, or Marple-bound, stopper. I wanted very badly to have a ride on one of those intriguing London expresses.

Even more frequent were trips to Oldham, every Saturday afternoon in the winter, when we used the train from Delph as the return adult fare was then 6d. as against 9d. on the bus, and you could be certain of a seat. There was a better bus service (just) true, but the Delph routes only saw single-deckers except for a solitary Oldham working operated by a double-decker to the Measurements factory for its workers at Monday to Friday evening finishing times. The single-deckers in the main had only 32 seats plus limited standing capacity, so the later ones were best avoided if one did not want to chance a six mile walk home. Our Saturday routine followed a set pattern. The 1.20 or 2.05 pm trains from Delph, arrive at Clegg Street 26 minutes later. Go to the cinema, and then have tea. Next visit relatives, where by chance an aunt of my mother and a married sister of my father lived within yards of each other in the Green Acres area. Now she had two sons of around my age, so when we went to their house I could be sure of playmates, but it was their father that I loved to meet, as he would talk to me, and answer all my questions. And so he deserves a chapter to himself, as he little knew just what influence those chats came to have upon me.

Finally, and as an aside, as we walked down the hill this time to Glodwick Road station for the 9.54 pm to Delph, we would see something that never happens these days. For we had to pass Townfield police station, and as we did, out would march a squad of officers led by a sergeant carrying a staff, who would be putting the night men onto their beats, and returning with the men they were to relieve.

Police constable 29, George Simmons of the Oldham Borough Force. This photograph was taken in 1919 after his demobilisation and start of police engagement, which was not of long duration. For the next three decades he was a Corporation tram or bus driver, passing away in hospital after an operation at the end of November 1954.

Chapter Three

Uncle George

Uncle George Simmons was a native of Cambridgeshire being born in March, where after leaving school he joined the former Great Eastern Railway in some very junior capacity. But his railway career was cut short by the outbreak of World War I when he enlisted in the army and saw service in France where he was badly wounded.

Brought back to 'Blighty' he was eventually sent to Oldham to recuperate, a rather surprising destination, as Oldham is not, and certainly was not then, a health resort. But no doubt after the trenches a convalescence in Werneth must have seemed like heaven. Whilst in the town he met one of my father's sisters, and on his discharge they were married, and in consequence he never went back to East Anglia.

Being a big man physically, an ex-serviceman and an ex-NCO, he was accepted as a constable in the then Oldham Borough Police Force, but had the misfortune to be involved in some fracas in the then notorious West Street area that aggravated his war wounds. His police engagement was cut short, but this did not mean the end of his municipal service as he almost instantly became a tram driver on the Corporation system without ever acting as a conductor.

He rapidly developed into a tram and bus enthusiast, and so gained a mine of information that he was more than ready to impart to me. This enthusiasm was perhaps all the more remarkable in view of the standards of discipline that were imposed on the staff in this period. Be late by more than a couple of minutes or even less and it was no work for the day, but if one was booked spare and no one missed a turn, again there would be no work, and no work meant no pay. Additionally when a staff member reported for duty he had to be sure that he was wearing full uniform with boots and buttons polished and of course wearing his cap.

No form of staff transport was provided so as the cars started running by five in the morning, and continued until midnight, walking to and from one's home was an absolute necessity. In uncle's case it was about 1¼ miles each way, and when you did report it was certain that your allocated tram would be one with an open front. Walking to work before five on a freezing Oldham winter morning, and then spending up to nine hours, there were no meal breaks, on the front of such a car, must have been no picnic. But all this was accepted in return for a wage of around £2 10s. per week, not a lot on which to support a family but vastly better than being unemployed. Thanks to the recession in the Oldham cotton industry all too many families were virtually on the breadline.

To see him on a wet day driving a car was another sight, and Oldham has more than its fair share of rain. Wearing an overcoat, plus a voluminous cape, and a waterproof cover on a well pulled down cap, he looked bigger than ever, but rain or no rain, time had to be kept. And here was another potential hazard, as it was a crime to put power on if the car was on a downwards slope that was sufficient of an incline to let gravity alone accelerate the car. Inspectors would lurk at

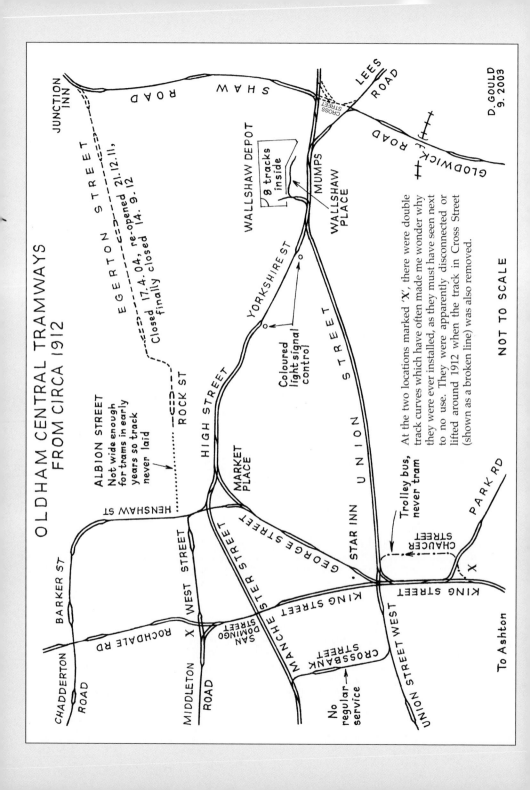

OLDHAM CENTRAL TRAMWAYS FROM CIRCA 1912

D. GOULD 9. 2003

NOT TO SCALE

JUNCTION INN

SHAW ROAD

LEES ROAD

CROSS STREET

GLODWICK ROAD

EGERTON STREET

Closed 17.4.04, re-opened 21.12.11, finally closed 14.9.12

WALLSHAW DEPOT

8 tracks inside

MUMPS

WALLSHAW PLACE

ALBION STREET
Not wide enough for trams in early years so track never laid

ROCK ST

YORKSHIRE ST

Coloured light signal control

HIGH STREET

UNION STREET

STAR INN

HENSHAW ST

MARKET PLACE

GEORGE STREET

MANCHESTER STREET

SAN DOMINGO STREET

Trolley bus, never tram

CHAUCER STREET

PARK RD

BARKER ST

CHADDERTON ROAD

ROCHDALE RD

WEST STREET

MIDDLETON ROAD

CROSSBANK STREET

KING STREET

KING STREET WEST

UNION STREET WEST

No regular service

To Ashton

X

X

X

At the two locations marked 'X', there were double track curves which have often made me wonder why they were ever installed, as they must have seen next to no use. They were apparently disconnected or lifted around 1912 when the track in Cross Street (shown as a broken line) was also removed.

suitable vantage points to check that this ruling was obeyed. If an infringement was spotted, and this was easy to see on open-fronted cars, suspension could well result. Uncle like all drivers liked some trams and disliked others, but one he really hated was No. 13 or 'Big Ben' as it was known to the staff. 'Big Ben' was new in 1901 and was then a bogie single-deck car in the series numbered 5-16. No. 4, one of the original batch of four experimental trams to be put in service when the first Middleton road route was opened in December 1900, was virtually identical. In 1903, however, Mr Wilkinson the then General Manager had No. 13 taken into the works and rebuilt as a double-decker still with open platforms but with straight staircases running inside the body. In this guise with a 72-seat capacity it remained in service until 1923, usage latterly being confined to rush hours, when it was usually to be seen carrying workers to or from Platt Brothers textile machinery works on Featherstall Road. The fact that No. 13 was a 'one off' leads one to conclude that it was in its new form by no means a success, and uncle often said that when fully laden it took some stopping, but that was in ye good old days - by 1923 they were well past.

One fateful day he and a colleague were detailed to take 'Big Ben' from Wallshaw Depot to Hollinwood works on its last journey for scrapping, so the two men tossed up for ends and uncle lost and boarded the front platform. Knowing that the brakes were not all they might be, he elected to travel via Union St, Ashton Road, and Hollins Road as these had much easier gradients than were to be found on the main double track route via Werneth. All went well until the loop after a length of double track by the Frederick Street junction. Here 'Big Ben' was travelling rather too fast, and then the rear bogie split the points and took the Oldham side 'up' rails so that any bystander witnessed 'Big Ben' travelling sideways down that part of Hollins Road. By good fortune nothing was coming up or waiting to pass, so it was with great relief that No. 13 finally reached its last resting place and two drivers returned whence they had come with a lot to talk about.

Uncle did not like the open balcony vestibuled cars either, Nos. 4-12, and 14-16 that were delivered new in 1921, the single-deckers having been withdrawn in 1916 and sold to Rotherham. The latter undertaking later resold eight to Walthamstow in 1919, the last survivors finally ending their careers in 1933 after passing into the ownership of the London Passenger Transport Board. There were also two other similar vestibuled open balcony cars, that had been rebuilt at Hollinwood, namely Nos. 34 and 45. According to uncle running caused air to be built up under the balcony roof, which was then forced down the stairs leaving a driver's left side in a perpetual draught which on a cold day was most unpleasant, and gave rise to various adverse side effects. He affirmed that an open-fronted car was much to be preferred and that during the years that he drove these vehicles he never suffered from a cold, those with Siemens equipment being his favourites, as they were fast trams.

Now several Oldham terminal tracks were located on downwards gradients, so entering them meant care. For example there was at Waterhead for years, several yards of marks in the tarmac beyond the end of the tracks to show where a Manchester Pilcher had done its best to try to reach Delph. A judicious use of the sand gear was desirable at such locations. Sometimes, though, the

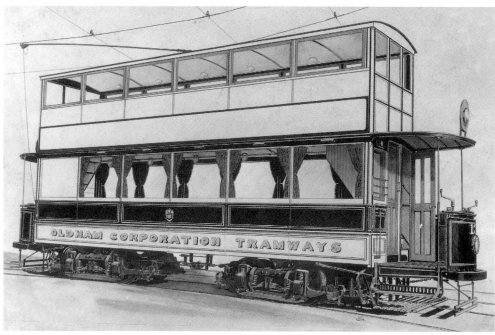

'Big Ben' was some tramcar being Oldham's second bogie double-decker and the only one with a covered top. The design was never repeated but it was unique for the time with its internal straight-run staircase. Driver protection and streamlining were conspicuous by their absence. No wonder Uncle George had a lot to say about it.

Oldham Market Place in the early 1900s. This was a 'lucky' photograph as car No. 34 standing close to a certain drinking fountain was the first tram to be fitted with a covered top in May 1904. Sadly this old commercial postcard has suffered over the years.

Car No. 99 of 1913 stands at the end of the track of Oldham's last 1913 tramway extension. The lines ended at the Shaw boundary but by the skyline is another boundary, that of Saddleworth. Denshaw is some 1½ miles away along the Halifax road. My family were delighted to see trams at this location these saving a mile walk to Moorside from 4th June, 1914. Car No. 99 had Siemens 40 hp motors and came into uncle's favourite category.

Right: In 1921 Oldham took delivery of 12 trams of this vestibuled open balcony design, Nos. 4 to 12 and 14 to 16. An existing tram, No. 45, was then rebuilt similarly, as later was No. 34. These were the trams Uncle George did not care for. Here No. 11 takes takes the right-hand curve into King Street but here in earlier years had been another unnecessary junction as a pair of left-hand curves led from Wellington Street to King Street. It would seem that these were lifted about 1912 when quite a lot of unwanted pointwork was eliminated.

This view of King Street at the Star Inn junction shows car No. 94 *en route* to Royton summit where one changed onto a Rochdale tram for that town. Note the hut for the boy who set the points at this location for cars travelling via King Street, Union Street, Union Street West and George Street, a task which kept him pretty busy in this period.

sand built up, when an incoming car would come to rest with sufficient sand under each of the four wheels to form a fully insulated negative return and no outward progress would be possible after power was put on. The remedy then was to borrow a bucket of water from an adjacent household, have the conductor lower the trolley, throw water round the wheels, return the trolley to the wire, and move off the sand. Why lower the trolley? Well failure to do so could result in some stimulating moments that once experienced were not easily forgotten. Some of that terminal line sand, however, could have been dropped not for stopping, but for a much darker purpose.

To take a car back to depot with a wheel flat was a hanging offence, but Oldham was in a very damp area, and there were numerous steep gradients so if a driver should have the misfortune to start a flat, was there a remedy? There was. Get to your remotest terminal point as quickly as possible, and once there cut out the motor to the good wheelset. Then both crew members screwed down the track brake as hard as possible so that the tram was almost lifted off the rails. Put the power on and as the damaged wheels revolved, feed sand under the tyre, this then acting as a grinding paste when, with careful use, the wheel could be trued up. All this did not do a lot for the health of the track, but as it took place on a single line terminal stub what matter?

In earlier years the track in Oldham was not too bad once most of the wartime arrears of maintenance had been made good. After the main line from Waterhead to Hollinwood via Werneth had been relaid with welded joints in the late 1920s it lasted with virtually no maintenance until the end of tramway service in August 1946, but the same could not be said of two foreign sections over which Oldham cars worked. The first of these was from the old Middleton Road terminus at the Chadderton boundary, through Chadderton itself to Mills Hill bridge, which was taken over by Oldham as its part of the assets of the former Middleton Electric Traction Company (MET) that had been acquired on 9th August, 1925. Along with the track came eight single truck open-fronted single-deckers that were from this time on used on a new Oldham service from Market Place (West Street top) to Middleton numbered 3, or on single morning and evening journeys over more rails now the property of Manchester tramways beyond Middleton to Rhodes. These journeys gave workers at the print works there who lived in the Chadderton area a through service previously provided by the MET. Uncle actually worked the very last trip of all to this 'distant' point in 1933. Oldham also worked a double-deck service over the Chadderton tracks as far as Mills Hill Bridge, such cars not being able to pass under that structure until it was rebuilt in December 1934. But double-deck workings through it were not of long duration as the whole route was closed on 10th June, 1935, by which time the ex-Middleton lines through Chadderton could almost be described as simply grooves in the highway's setted surface. If their condition was bad there were worse to be negotiated and these were the old Oldham, Ashton and Hyde lines from the Hathershaw boundary into Ashton Market Place. These formed part of the share of that concern's undertaking that passed to Ashton Corporation in 1921 and then on 2nd July, 1921 a through service between the two towns was begun, No. 14, the Oldham terminus being located at Star Inn.

Oldham Market Place looking in the westerly direction. Car No. 34 is in the process of gaining the top of George Street - now covered by the Spindles Centre. No. 34, originally open-topped and rebuilt to the form shown in 1922 is heading to Grains Bar after travelling via Hollins from Hollinwood. This tram lasted until the end of 1939.

In 1922 Mr Thorpe, the rolling stock superintendent, had cars Nos. 40 and 54 rebuilt to a fully enclosed form. Six new trams to a similar general design followed being built by English Electric in 1924 and numbered 17, 18, 19, 20, 22 and 24. Here is No. 24 on the four-track layout at Hollinwood. Nos. 19 and 20 were scrapped in 1939 the other survived until 1946 when Gateshead Tramways bought 17, 18 and 24

Uncle George soon found himself driving on this route, and was not impressed. So bad was the condition of the ex-company rail that Oldham would only allocated open-topped cars to the service and, as not all of these had balconies, the unfortunate driver became wetter than ever on rainy days. As George said, get a full jug of tea at Hathershaw and thanks to the rough ride by Bardsley most of the contents would be spilled on the platform.

To make matters worse, not only did the Ashton undertaking buy sufficient new cars to cover all the former company routes, including the joint workings to Oldham, but the associated expenditure also saw piles of new rails that were positioned at various places between Ashton and Hathershaw and then were never laid.

As it was, the joint service lasted until 26th August, 1925, when at Ashton's behest single-deck trolleybuses took over. Oldham purchased two of these machines, keeping them in a former tram shed located in the Corporation yard, at the top of Hollins Road, and wiring up Chaucer Street at Star Inn to provide a suitable loop for terminal purposes, and, of course, stringing up new wiring from Star Inn along Ashton Road to Hathershaw to accommodate this new form of transport. However, the Oldham trolleybus innovation was not to last long. Thanks to their unladen weight and solid tyres they produced more vibration on the granite-setted roads than the trams ever did and loud was the chorus of complaints that swelled from local residents. So on 5th September, 1926 Oldham jettisoned its share of the route and put trams back onto the Hathershaw-Summit route from which they had been withdrawn on 2nd April, 1926.

Uncle George never did become a trolleybus driver, but by 1933 consideration was being given to the complete abandonment of tramway operations. He was selected for motor bus driver training, and thus came to experience the infamous Guy and Karrier six-wheelers in both single- and double-deck forms, as they were approaching the end of their lives. Sadly, a little before he moved over from railed vehicles the undertaking, in an attempt to effect economies, removed the self-starters from all petrol-engined buses. At this time there was only one oil-engined machine in the fleet, fitted as an experiment to Leyland Titan No. 72, of the batch 68-75, then only about nine months old. It will be readily understood that if a driver did stall an engine whilst out on the road, he certainly needed to be strong in the arm, and sufficiently aware of what might happen if he did not remember to retard the ignition before swinging the handle. This, though, was only one problem he now had to face. Of the others, the bus garage from 1926 had been on Oldham Edge at least another mile from his home, and whilst all the buses did have windscreens, that did not automatically mean that drivers kept dry. Older vehicles had fully floating cabs that were interesting in that the front and sides of these structures were not secured to the roof. Between these two essential parts were rubber strips, only these naturally perished or tore, so on entering the cab on a wet day, the driver took off his overcoat and hung it on the windward side, otherwise he would experience frequent showers.

The cabs too were by no means handy. Electric horns were not incorporated, so to give warning of one's approach a rubber bulb had to be squeezed hard, but as that bulb was just behind the front dashplate George, despite his considerable height, had to rise from his seat to reach it. Add to that the possibility of petrol

This is one of a series of pictures taken by W.A. Camwell at the door of the now demolished Wallshaw tram depot, Oldham. The driver of car No. 11 in anticipation of that draught coming down the stairs wears his overcoat and scarf while his colleague on No. 129 is content to be in a tunic. The badge on the left sleeve of his mate denotes 10 years' continuous service. A star above the badge meant 15 years, another below meant 20 years, Uncle George was proud of his. The managerial offices were right above this doorway.

Car No. 49, originally an open-topper, underwent two rebuildings, the last one producing the result shown here. Originally intended to be the prototype of an envisaged modernisation programme it remained with lower saloon transverse seats in solitary splendour until withdrawal at the end of 1939. This view on the No. 8 Shaw-Hollinwood route was taken when completed in late 1931. Note the truck cover. Two other Oldham trams in the 121-132 series were similarly fitted but none remained *in situ* for more than a few years.

starvation on a long hill, as usage exceeded the amount that the Autovac could provide, and throw in all too many breakdowns and a driver's lot in fair weather could be more than a mite interesting. Winter was another matter when a combination of icy roads, stone sets, two rear axles and air brakes that were not exactly of the fully proportional form could and did give rise to sliding Karriers. He fascinated me on one occasion by telling me how he had slid sideways down the Delph road below Scouthead almost to Wall Hill.

He continued to drive buses until the early days of World War II, but was involved in a blackout accident when a motorcyclist was badly injured. Exonerated from any blame he took an indoor job on nights for a time, but then went back to the front end and now and then found himself back tram driving on the sole surviving Waterhead to Hollinwood and Manchester route that should have closed in September 1939, but thanks to the war remained until August 1946.

Towards the end of World War II the 27 remaining trams were not in the best of condition, and it seems that as a result of the braking strains involved he had to undergo an operation. From then onwards his health deteriorated, and so he had to retire, when his condition continued to slowly worsen. I would go and see him as often as I could, and he would tell me more about his past experiences, and inquire also as to my progress in the transport industry, telling me to keep at it and then he would soon see me as a General Manager.

Alas, though, that was never to be. On the day I came back from Halifax having been appointed head of the engineering department, I left my bus at Hill Stores and went to his home to find he was back in hospital, and had that very day undergone yet another operation, passing away from its effects the same night so I was never able to tell him that I really now was on the way.

I can here pay tribute to his memory, for he was a great friend, whose interest and stories fired the ambition that was within one, and helped to convince me that I too wanted to be in municipal transport, with my name on the side of the vehicles, along with those magic words 'General Manager'. But I was also attracted to railways, thanks no doubt to those BDV smoking coupons, and it did not seem possible that one could ever gain experience in both modes of transport.

Acquired for just 260 BDV coupons I still have my Bassett Lowke 4-4-0 tender locomotive *Princess Elizabeth*, although the cast driving wheels are corroding with age.

The last new trams for Oldham were the 12 English Electric vehicles, Nos. 121 to 132, delivered in 1926. They were unique at the time, being fitted with upholstered seats throughout. All lasted until the end of the system in 1946. Here No. 123 stands on the Grains Bar route in front of the Wagon & Horses Inn above Moorside when brand new. The wall in the background still survives but the fields behind are now largely covered by the post-war Sholver estate.

These examples of the author's ration books date from the post-war period.

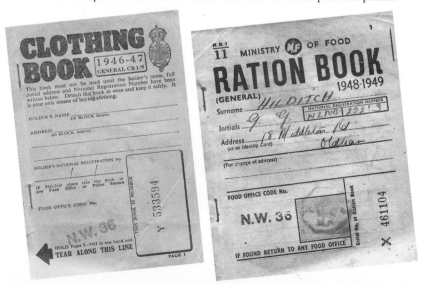

Chapter Four

Hobson's Choice

In January 1939 the depression in the calico printing industry caught up with father once more and he lost his job. Alternative work in his profession as colourist simply did not exist and so in order to survive the parents purchased a mixed (very mixed) business in what was then possibly the poorest part of Oldham, a decision that, in view of what was to come in the following September, turned out to be quite advantageous.

Living as we now did in an area where common lodging houses and back-to-back dwellings with atrocious sanitation provisions abounded, one could not fail to be struck by the abysmal poverty that was everywhere to be seen. Although it must be said that many of our customers were real characters, and very honest ones at that. Having little money they had to be careful with their purchases so the request for 'sid ricks and a pennorth of "rootie"' was a common occurrence. This meant a cone-shaped sweet bag, small size, filled with a mixture of sugar and cheap tea, together with five slices of bread off a sliced loaf that then cost complete just 4½d. The other frequent purchase was a 1d. Nelson cake. We obtained most of our confectionery from a Warrington-based concern that delivered daily and in the process would take back anything unsold during the previous 24 hours. This by some mysterious process was then reconstituted into the aforementioned Nelson cake that was about the volume of one third of a standard brick and perchance was of the same consistency. I was never brave enough to tackle one but was of the firm opinion that not only could they stop the proverbial 'gob' but also a runaway tramcar.

We were like an establishment of BBC tv fame, open all hours, initially from 6.00 am to 10.00 pm, but when the war and blackout came these hours were dramatically reduced although some evening trade remained with the earlier closing of the cinemas. This reduction made life easier in some respects but rationing brought new chores. Tinned goods and sweets, etc. were on points which had to be cut out from a book and then carefully saved. Once a month all these had to be counted and placed in hundreds in a small envelope that was then enclosed in a larger official one and on the front the shop keeper had to declare how many points in total were included.

A voucher would be sent in return to enable replacement supplies to be obtained. The staff in the Food Office would routinely open the big envelopes, take out the small ones, open one or two and count the contents and heart stopping inquiries would follow should any discrepancy be found. It can be said at this distance of time that the lodging house residents were not sartorial dressers or sweet eaters, so coupon exchanges that came to benefit the involved parties were not unknown.

We sold cigarettes (Wills Woodbines 10 for 4d., or Players 10 for 6d. or 20 for 11½d.), but not, rather strangely, my father's favourite pipe tobacco, which meant my going to a nearby specialist shop when his stock needed replenishment. One day whilst so engaged I broke off my purchasing activities

After 1932 there were no more new North Western Tilling Stevens buses. The company bought some Leyland and Dennis-based buses then in 1936 purchased Bristol JOG5 chassis and 31-seat rear entrance Eastern Coach Works bodies. This combination then formed the North Western standard to wartime years. They were noisy and vibrated despite their luxurious interiors until the driver engaged overdrive. Then there was a satisfying 'clonk' when speed with quietness reigned.

Shortly after I started at Oldham Grammar school in September 1937 my parents bought me a bicycle. Late in March 1938 I rode it to Stalybridge, found the depot and was surprised to find nine trams in it. None were apparent on the streets, but there were tracks with wires. So why? W.A. Camwell supplied the answer some years later when he sent me this photograph he took on 18th September, 1937. The trams then ran peak periods only on Stalybridge-Albion Hotel-Hyde, Stalybridge-Park Road-Dukinfield-Hyde and Stalybridge-Millbrook. One open-topper, No. 47, still survived at this time. An official SHMD map of the period in my possession confirms the foregoing. In 1937 no trams ran beyond Acres Lane/Mottram Road but in 1936 all the Mottram Road tracks were shown as being extant.

to hasten to the door to watch one of the older open-fronted trams pass. The proprietor asked me why the interruption, and after I had replied with the reason, asked a second question, 'Would you like a bus book?' On saying 'Please, yes', he vanished into the rear of his premises to return with a copy of the then publication *Passenger Transport*. Subsequently, and for some years too, he passed his copy on to me usually quite unopened and contained in its postal container. The address on the wrapper told me that my beneficiary was an Alderman of the Borough Council and also Vice-Chairman of the local transport committee, but the real significance of that office then quite escaped me.

These journals gave an insight into what was then happening in the transport field and what so many of the senior figures in the industry really looked like. But I never imagined that in another 15 years or so I would not only know many of the younger ones personally, but also be able to address them by their Christian names.

To return to the shop. The living accommodation was much better than one might have expected for premises with a rent of 12 shillings a week, even if we did have electric lighting downstairs and gas up, but there were electric plugs on the top deck, and room to increase the size of my model railway. By early 1940 I had managed to acquire some gems such as Hornby and Bassett Lowke locomotives that represented the better end of their catalogue offerings, but then supplies became unavailable and so for the next six years I was lucky if I could find some suitable second-hand items. Something that came in this category was a German made 20 volt ex-Midland Railway LMS 4-4-0 and three matching clerestory coaches, but, alas, I only had a very limited amount of track and points so it only had a limited use. Another purchase that had no use at all was a Hornby Metropolitan Railway electric locomotive and the fearsome controller that went with it. This required the services of a light bulb that fitted into a holder mounted on the top of the casing. This was far too scary for me, so it never did run, but looked decorative when standing in a siding. Some electric development was to be seen on our main streets, however, very early in September.

Only a very few days after the outbreak of World War II, a day that found me travelling back from Newcastle on a Tyne-Tees-Mersey express bus and running into the strange blacked-out world after we had passed through Dewsbury, Oldham buses were turned out with very reduced exterior and interior lighting, with blue painted windows for good measure. This gave very restricted visibility, but a day or so later I became certain that I had passed an impossibility whilst riding on one, the impossibility being a repainted tram, but I had. Thanks to Adolf Hitler the No. 47 tramway replacement buses numbers 180 to 226 were put into store in the Wallshaw Garage as they came to be delivered from the Leeds works of body builders Chas H. Roe, and the trams left to continue in peace but not for long. In the meantime, however, the last new trams Nos. 121 to 132 *did* have a quick repaint only the gloss very soon faded, then they looked shabbier than ever. At this time just after the war had begun the tram fleet was 44 strong including the rebuilt car No. 49, and my favourite No. 112. This tram had begun life in 1900 as an open-topped double-deck bogie car, the only such tram ever purchased new by Oldham, it being one

On 6th November, 1937 two more tram services came to an end, namely the No. 4 circular route and No. 7 Hathershaw-Star Inn-Royton-Summit workings. Here Chamberlain car No. 128 stands at Hathershaw, the 12 members of this series being regular route 7 performers. From 1921 to 25th August, 1925 trams had continued beyond Hathershaw to the right on the joint service to Ashton. On 26th August trolleybuses took over until 5th September, 1926 when a full Oldham to Hathershaw tram service was restored. Ashton continued to run trolleybuses to Hathershaw until 19th February, 1939, their terminal loop being at the end of the row of houses on the right. With these closures the fleet was reduced to 44 trams, nine retaining open fronts. No. 128 later became No. 70 in the Gateshead fleet.

To replace the trams on routes 4 and 7 more new buses were required. Leyland obtained most of the chassis orders (for 35 'TD5' models) but the body order was split, Nos. 132 to 152 having English Electric coachwork. Here Nos. 146 and 147 stand in Wallshaw garage. They lasted until 1948/1954 but were not up to the standard of the 15 Roe bodies, Nos. 153 to 167, that came into stock in the same period, and after the war 21 were rebuilt mainly by outside contractors.

of the four original and experimental cars with which operations were begun. Oldham, though, never took to bogies and so in 1915 as the eight-wheeled single-deckers were being sold to Rotherham No. 3, as it then was, also came to be withdrawn. The body was installed in the Glodwick Road permanent way yard and used as a store.

In 1921 as new cars were in short supply the carcass was taken into the works, and reduced in length by one bay, i.e. from six to five. Non-standard four window top cover was added, as were stairs, the platforms, and a four-wheeled truck and the end result emerged to take the rails once more as open-fronted No. 112. It looked odd especially as by now the platforms had begun to droop, and was only to be seen on rush hour work, as were the other remaining open-front cars, but even in old age one of these showed me just how destructive a tram could be.

Each evening several old timers would leave the shed at Mumps and travel down Manchester Street to Werneth; here they would reverse, use the cross-over and then make their way into Featherstall Road to provide transport for workers leaving the extensive premises of Platt Brothers textile machinery factory. On the night in question I was just below the San Domingo Street traffic lights watching what was in the convoy. 'Tail end Charlie' being rather behind its fellows was descending Manchester Street somewhat faster than was normally the case, and as the traffic lights were showing green the driver made no attempt to slow down which turned out to be rather unfortunate.

One block below the lights a side street, Eagle Street, crossed Manchester Street, the north side of this coming from West Street, the south side running behind the extensive King Street premises of the Co-operative Society, and containing the cartage department of that same enterprise. As I watched a coal wagon came smartly out of the northern section after what must have been a busy day, as the carter was asleep on his box, and the horse thinking of its stable and evening meal was not about to stop for anything let alone a tram.

The driver of that vehicle put on the emergency brake, and dropped copious amounts of sand but all to no avail. The tram hit the coal wagon fair and square between the wheels, there was an almighty crash and the air was filled with a dense cloud of vintage coal dust of which the driver had his fair share too. The end result was interesting. The rear wheels, tailboard, and some splintered planks lay on my side of Manchester Street, whilst more planks, and the carter occupied the opposite pavement, the latter now somewhat shaken and giving vent to some language that was not exactly of the drawing room variety. The horse complete with shafts and front wheels was a speck in the distance as it headed for home, and the tram, now stationary some three or four lengths down the road, was quite unscathed, whilst the driver rather resembled the late Al Jolson when in stage make up. Such scenes came to an end on 3rd December, 1939 when the Long Shaw to Hollinwood via Werneth route closed, and with it went 17 trams including Nos. 49 and 112, plus a 1921 vestibuled car No. 7, two 1924 totally enclosed cars Nos. 19 and 20, Oldham rebuilds Nos. 34, 40, 45 and 54, and the last of the other open-fronted cars Nos. 29, 30, 31, 41, 53, 75, 78 and 94.

Now when in 1937 the circular route closed the track and overhead were left in from Mumps Bridge to the Glodwick permanent way yard, it being the

In 1937 Oldham took delivery of six Daimler/Roe 54-seat double-deckers, Nos. 168 to 173. They had Gardner '6LW' engines, the only ones they ever owned. They were initially allocated to the Chapel Road-Greenacres service, so from then all rides to or from Hulme Grammar School were by smooth running pre-selector-geared Daimlers. They must have given satisfaction for in 1939 a batch of Daimler single-deckers was ordered, but due to the start of the war the never were delivered. Here is No. 172, after completion at the Crossgates, Leeds works of the body builder.

Six more Leylands, Nos. 174 to 179, were obtained in 1938, this batch having the later style of Leyland 56-seat all metal bodywork. Much more successful than the 102-104 series, they lasted until 1952. Here No. 179 stands in Peter Street - now completely covered by the Spindles shopping centre.

intention to scrap the remaining trams there as they were taken out of service, but despite this retention these 17 unfortunates met their end not at Glodwick but at Manchester's Hyde Road Depot. I have a reminder of No. 112 still in my possession in the form of one of its destination blinds, and it is something of a shock to realise that I have had it now for over 60 years.

To provide for this conversion some of the new buses came out of store, and so one morning when on my way to Star Inn and school No. 189 passed me heading towards Hathershaw. I ran, caught it and booked to the terminus as I had to have a ride on this new marvel, which made me late and was a dangerous thing to do in that day of the cane or punishment drill. If 189 had an adverse effect on my education much worse ones came to be encountered when rather older buses were very much to blame. The area where the Oldham Technical College now stands was then an open space officially called Ward Park, but known locally as 'The Brews'. As Bent Hall was still standing, although now split into several down-market dwellings, it must once have been a pleasant area, but those days were now long past. For industry had come and gone. At our end were the surviving buildings of Dura Mill, and then the ruins of what had once been Dowry Mill, with the massive dam wall of that enterprise now breached to keep it dry. Then came two streets of very mean houses, namely Newlands Street and Portland Street, the latter having direct access to Rochdale Road. The middle of the Brews had once been the site of a coal mine and part of the cobbled road that led to it was still *in situ*, but where the pit head once was now lay an almost level portion that despite its ash/cinder surface was used as a football pitch. Elsewhere were humps, bumps, and paths that provided me with cycling pleasure, but one day I found that at the foot of Portland Street a large notice had been erected which said 'Dead slow' and had a red arrow pointing to the right beneath this instruction. The next day a wooden hut mounted on wheels was positioned at one side of the 'park' but just what was the reason?

After tea the following Monday I found out when, with a rattle and roar, a Corporation double-decker came down Portland Street, turned the corner, and was then directed where to park by a man who came out of the hut on hearing of its approach. Within the hour 39 more had followed, for we were now in the period of the blitz, and so dispersal was the name of the game. For the record another 40 found lodgings every night in some then spare ground at the junction of Chamber Road with Ashton Road, but these did not concern me.

In no time at all I had opened up diplomatic relations with Bill and Joe, and so became an honorary staff member. The drill was the same every night. Remove every steering wheel to immobilise the buses, this being easily done by a tommy bar arrangement located in the centre of the wheel. Make sure every main switch was off, turn every destination blind to blank, and ensure every opening window, mainly of the half-drop pattern, was closed, leave the gear lever in neutral and, when cool, check radiator levels, plus those of the sump. This was all fascinating stuff, but better was to follow. The buses stayed out from after the peak lunch time workings on Saturday to early Monday morning, and Bill and Joe spent some of their weekend hours on duty as a consequence. One Saturday when all was quiet Bill Howard elected to give me my first

I always enjoyed a ride on a Manchester 'Pilcher' as some of the 38-strong series were equipped with track brakes and so could work on the No. 20 route to Oldham and Waterhead. This one is approaching the King Street/Manchester Street junction. The Aldermanic owner of the right-hand shop was the gentleman who gave me those *Passenger Transport* magazines. Right behind the car is the street out of which came a certain coal cart. As built 'Pilchers' would have been better had a longer wheelbase truck been fitted. Leeds City Transport did just this to one of its second-hand ex-Manchester purchases with beneficial results. The truck was an EMB flexible axle product, car No. 281.

The Transport Department planned to close its last two tramway routes in late 1939 and so ordered its biggest batch of buses to date, 47 Leyland 'TD5' chassis and a like number of teak-framed Roe bodies, Nos. 180 to 226 inclusive. Due to the outbreak of war the trams continued, but it was possible to close the No. 8 Shaw-Royton-Hollinwood service in December 1939 when buses Nos. 180-199 entered service. The rest followed in four batches from August 1940 to January 1941. They proved to be a fortuitous acquisition. Here is No. 189, which made me late for school on first sighting.

driving lesson, but what Mr Richards the then General Manager would have thought about this is not to be contemplated here. As it was Bill told me a lot and not just about buses for he had in the past been employed at a place called Gorton Tank, and so we covered locomotive matters as well.

Now it so happened that I could by this time expect a very friendly reception at another and rather different hut, not in Lancashire, but in Yorkshire, thanks to the good sense of my father's younger brother, of smoking fame. He had not only moved to Doncaster, but had also taken up residence in close proximity to a couple of LNER main lines. It was only a short walk from his home to Moat Hills and Dock Hills crossings where the lane they served passed across the tracks from Doncaster to Leeds and to York. There was plenty to see, and do, because those crossings about 150 yards apart found employment for Mr Thomas Exelby who worked alternate early and late turns, and Mr Frank Bennett who with his family occupied the crossing keeper's house and guarded the gates when Tom was away from duty. A former Great Eastern man, Mr Bennett had transferred after Grouping to Wath Yard as a shunter, but had slipped one day, while so engaged, and lost a leg as a consequence. He was, though, very active having a cycle with one loose pedal to take his false leg's foot, and a fixed gear, and so going from one set of gates to the other was of little trouble to him.

Both men recognised my interest, and quickly accepted my visits as a matter of course, soon showing me how when the needles showed 'line clear' to ring Marshgate box and ask for Leeds and York. Then the locking lever in each hut had to be pulled over, and when the button under the locking box on each gate had been pressed, the bolt could be slid back and the gate opened. There was also a closing procedure to be followed.

Between them they told me a great deal about railways in general, and their various careers up to that time, and showed me such things as trains went past as brake vans with concrete sides, or the 'bomb badges' on the sides of ex-North Eastern good engines that had served in France during World War I.

This was not the only bonus. I made frequent trips to Doncaster, sometimes by bus sampling a variety of routes, or more often by train, when my cycle could go with me. Such a journey meant a bike ride to Clegg Street station, and a trip on the Guide Bridge push-and-pull local service that up to the outbreak of the war had been quite frequent but then was greatly reduced. At Guide Bridge I changed onto a Sheffield train, some going on to London with a Pacific at their head, then another change could follow at Sheffield unless I had picked up a through Liverpool to Hull train at Guide Bridge. Now I really was seeing more LNER engines than had ever previously been the case, and my notebook began to be filled with new names and numbers. It was a series of ex-Great Central engines that took my fancy, with 'Directors' and Atlantics being firm favourites, whilst the 'B7' class locomotives had a beefy look to them. I did not then realise that in not too many years I would have a much closer (too close?) association with them.

I then discovered that the return journey could be made via any recognised route, and this happy realisation offered wider horizons. I was enabled to catch an LNER train to Leeds Central, often hauled by an ex-GCR 4-6-0, and there

Left: I put in this gorgeous picture of Karrier No. 43 at the Iron Railings as it shows the rubber sealing strip below the cab roof, for the cabs were of the fully floating pattern. To ensure he kept dry, as the rubber tore or perished, Uncle George hung his greatcoat over the door when he encountered an Oldham monsoon. On hot days the gaps produced useful ventilation as the petrol engines produced a considerable amount of heat. No. 43 was one of six new in 1928.

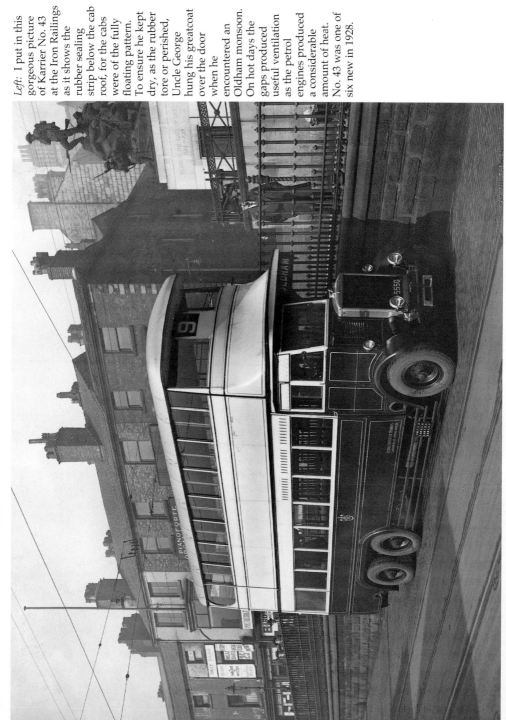

Delph station from the buffer stops looking towards Oldham. From September 1937 I travelled daily on the train to Oldham Clegg Street when four coaches and a push-and-pull-fitted Webb 'Coal Tank' formed the usual make-up. The Fowler 2-6-2 tanks came on the scene in 1938 after displacement by the Wirral area electrification scheme. After the war thanks to the fall in the number of passengers two-coach sets as shown here became the norm.

change to an LMS train for Rochdale travelling via Halifax. I could then either ride home from Rochdale if the weather was good, or use a local train to Oldham Central, a station like Clegg Street now long closed. Another and more attractive alternative was to cross to City station in Leeds, leave the cycle in the parcels office, have a tram ride or two, and then use the Huddersfield to Greenfield route, and so come to complete my trip home from Greenfield on the Delph donkey, a service I had previously used daily on my journeys to or from Oldham Grammar School.

If I did use this latter route one thing always struck me, and that was how much the frontal appearance of a Leeds pivotal car resembled the front of one of the Oldham 1924 totally enclosed cars, or the very similar Hollinwood rebuilds. In fact the first of the pivotals with its different destination equipment was here identical, but as I found out later there was no surprise involved as the Leeds drawing office files contained Oldham drawings, these dating from the time of Mr Chamberlain who had managed both undertakings. The pivotals did not impress me. Horsfields and Middleton bogies came in my estimation into a very different category, and as the Middleton cars stopped so close to City station what could be nicer than a tram ride through the woods?

There were two rail rides I never was able to take. Just after noon struck a Doncaster to York stopping train passed the crossing usually made up of three ex-North Eastern clerestory coaches and hauled by an elderly 4-4-0. Whilst just after 4.00 pm came a through train from York to Colchester headed by an ex-GCR 4-6-0 from Lincoln with a very long string of stock behind the tender. I fancied a trip on both but neither was possible. Thanks to my crossing keeper friends and my cycle I did locate other things of interest, namely the complete but disused station at Sprotborough, the two ex-Dearne & District tram bodies still in original livery and joined end-on that now formed a cycle shop in Bolton-upon-Dearne and finally the Dearne Valley Light Railway, with its ex-Lancashire & Yorkshire Railway (LYR) railmotors running from Edlington to Wakefield. Only when I did take a trip on it the railmotor must have been having an off day.

Fortunately there were other treats too numerous to detail, for thanks to numerous relatives and the strong visiting tradition within the family nicely spread out from London in the South via Birmingham to Newcastle in the North, I managed to see lots of locomotives, scores of buses of different makes, had tram rides in 'foreign parts' where a run in Birmingham to Rednal or Rubery (routes first seen in 1938) always filled in a pleasant afternoon, and felt myself very lucky as a result.

Now, though, I was reaching the age when a decision had to be made about what I was going to do in the days to come. The war situation for this country had looked brighter after Hitler sent his legions to march into Russia, and the Japanese had had their 'day of infamy' on 7th December, 1941. But there was obviously still a long way to go before hostilities came to an end, and thanks to my evening stints with those buses my school attainments were not exactly all that could be desired, even if I did manage to pass the school certificate exams. It was time to leave Hulme Grammar School and find a job, which obviously had to be in the transport industry.

Consequently I set about the task of writing letters of application in my neatest hand to all the local bus companies, both private and municipally owned, enclosing stamped addressed envelopes in the hopes of at least receiving a reply. But when they came disappointment was the order of the day. Not one of them had any form of opening, not even as a parcel boy, for an aspiring General Manager, so it was a case of 'Hobson's Choice', and if the buses would not have me perhaps a railway company would. I did in later years have a little satisfaction in indicating to local and more senior members of the Municipal Passenger Transport Association what a treasure they had missed back in 1942; I gathered that missing me then was not a matter of regret to them.

I then wrote to the LMS and LNER, and the former replied first, telling me to report to the Hunts Bank, Manchester offices for interview. I duly did so, and was not impressed by what followed. Several applicants including myself were marshalled by a very supercilious staff clerk into a far from pleasant room at the top of the building, and there given a series of tests. At the end of the day I left for home via the Oldham train on my free ticket sure in the knowledge that I did *not* want to work for the LMS, so now the LNER was my last remaining hope.

The company came up trumps.

A nice letter arrived asking me to go to Doncaster for an interview with another free ticket enclosed. So some days before the date indicated I caught the

9.16 am from Clegg Street, changing onto the 9.45 am from Manchester to Marylebone at Guide Bridge and taking my cycle with me. I had more spells at the crossings with my two friends, and at the appointed time found myself in a bright room at the south end of Doncaster station sitting in front of a panel of about four gentlemen headed by a Mr Taylor who was obviously a man of some authority. I was asked more questions, and some of these related to railway geography, and here luck came my way again. In the course of an early 1940 journey to see some relatives we had to cross from Manchester Victoria to Exchange station, and on the bookstall there I saw a *Railway Magazine*. I persuaded my parents to part with a shilling, and have taken the publication ever since. I always read my early ones from cover to cover, and I had often purchased a copy of *Bradshaw* so I managed to survive what could have been quite an ordeal fairly easily and was given a reward as a consequence.

Mr Taylor presented me with a short list of junior clerks jobs that were then available in the Manchester area, and then asked me which one I would like. There was no contest here. The district locomotive superintendent's office Gorton stuck out like a sore thumb so my name was duly inscribed against those almost magic words.

Mr Taylor then asked how had I managed to make Doncaster for an early morning interview so I told him where I had been staying. He then asked me for my travel ticket, and my initial letter, and wrote on both, handing them back to me with a smile and saying, 'Now you can stay with your relatives until the end of the month if you wish'. What a difference to Hunts Bank it all was. The LNER and locomotives - it all seemed too good to be true. My return home, though, was a very different matter indeed.

On what was to be my last night at my aunt's I went to the cinema, and during the course of the film felt a pain in my right side, which got worse during the night. My train to Guide Bridge was late, the Oldham train had gone, so I mounted my cycle intending to ride home, and ride I did staying in the saddle all the way from the foot of Bardsley Brow through Hathershaw to the shop door, By now, thanks to the strain imposed by pedalling up the intervening gradients, what had been a grumbling appendix had become a very nasty one, and I almost collapsed over the counter.

There was now awaiting me another letter telling me to report to my chosen place of employment just a few days later. But instead of going to Gorton. I went into the local hospital for an operation and felt very shaky for quite a time after my eventual discharge. But my parents' letter of explanation received a kind reply which said the job was still open to me, and I was to report just as soon as I was able. I always thought that the LNER was 'The Gentleman's Railway', this surely proved the case.

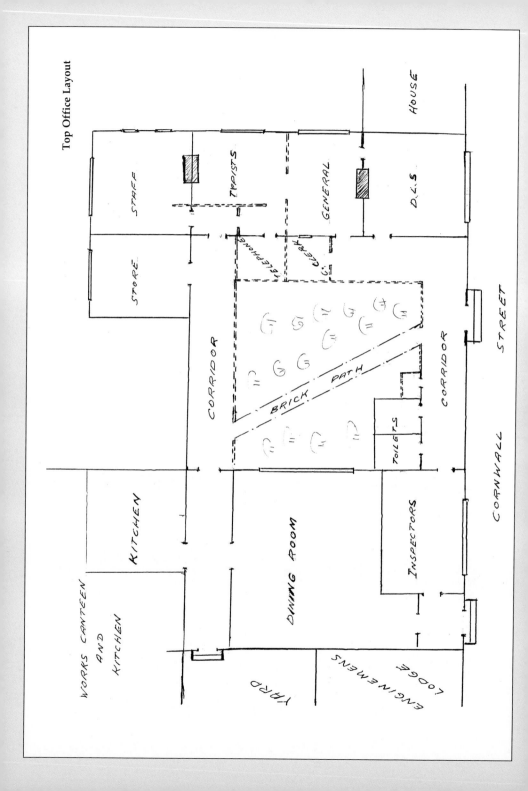

Top Office Layout

Chapter Five

The Top Office

It took me several weeks to recover from the operation and its after-effects, but early in December I felt well enough to catch the 9.16 am from Oldham Clegg Street station to Guide Bridge, where I changed onto another 'C13' class 4-4-2T-powered local and so came to alight from my GCR vintage non-corridor coach at Gorton and Openshaw station.

For the first time I walked up the sloping path from the platforms to the booking office, and then after asking my way, along the path that ran along the top of the railway retaining wall and over the footbridge spanning the Stockport branch of the Ashton canal to Cornwall Street. My walk continued along that thoroughfare until I came on the right-hand side to a door set in an almost blank wall besides which was a polished brass plate bearing the inscription 'LNER District Locomotive Superintendent'. I walked up the steps and through the door to find myself confronted with a corridor about 6 ft wide, glazed above the waist on the side away from the door, whilst straight ahead was a door leading to what might loosely be called a garden. This led, I was to find later, to a passage at the back of the office and a rear door thereto where Mrs Patrickson produced coffee and tea for the staff and where Jimmy Mayall, the office messenger who was a casualty of World War I, spent his spare time. To the left of me now was another door and to the right a right-angled bend in the corridor. I took the latter to find myself facing not one door but three, two of which were marked 'Private'. The middle one was labelled 'Inquiries' so I knocked and waited but not for long, being quickly ushered into the office where I would in a few days be working. First, though, I was taken to be interviewed by the chief clerk, then a Mr Sayers, a man of about 50 or so wearing a brown suit which was his normal attire. His office lay behind the door marked 'private' which had been in front of me. This meant his 'room' was in effect an extension of that corridor and was accordingly quite narrow having a window which gave a view of the general office that I had first entered.

After asking a few questions, he told me that the offices under his control were in two parts dealing with staff and general matters respectively and I was to be posted to the latter whose head was a Mr Rowbottom. I was taken and introduced to him, a tall gentleman with grey hair who was as pleasant as I could expect, and whom I later discovered lived of all places in Disley. He was a long serving ex-GCR man whose father had been station master at Harwarden Bridge back in pre-GCR days. I then met the other members of his staff, George Gregory his second in command, Mr Hockram, Mr and Mrs Clappison, Miss Ennever and Fred Kemp, and then four typists.

Next came a visit to the staff section headed by Mr Barber, when it all seemed suspiciously like starting at a new school. A feeling that was heightened by the whole of the buildings, for these premises had been built by the railway company as a school in Victorian days to educate the children of the men working at Gorton; and so the class room origin of these offices was only too

Timetable for Guide Bridge, Ashton and Stalybridge trains, 1st May, 1939 to 2nd July, 1939.

Table 75

GUIDE BRIDGE, ASHTON, and STALYBRIDGE

Week Days

Miles		mrn	mrn	mrn	mrn	mrn	mrn S		aft S	aft S	aft S	aft	aft		aft E	aft E	aft E		aft	aft S				
	80 MANCHESTER (Cen.) dep	..	..	..	7 43	8A25	1122	..	..	12A10	..	..	..	..	4 28	..	5 43	..	7 22	..	..	..	..	..
	77 " (Lon. Rd.) "	6 5	6 58	7 33	8 5	8 43	1130	..	1211	12 27	1 10	3 15	4 20	..	5 3	5 49	6 10	..	7 25	1015	..	..	..	..
—	Guide Bridge dep	6 26	7 18	7 47	8 22	9 6	1152	..	1229	12 55	1 30	3 33	4 40	..	5 23	6 3	6 29	..	7 50	1032	..	..	..	..
¾	Dukinfield	6 29	7 21	7 50	8 24	9 9	1155	..	1232	12 58	1 32	3 36	4 43	..	5 26	6 6	6 32	..	7 53	1035	..	..	..	..
1¼	Ashton (Park Parade)	6 33	7 23	7 53	8 27	9 12	1158	..	1234	1 1	1 35	3 38	4 47	..	5 29	6 10	6 35	..	7 56	1037	..	..	..	..
2½	Stalybridge arr	6 37	7 27	7 57	8 30	9 16	12 2	..	1237	1 5	1 38	3 41	4 51	..	5 32	6 14	6 39	..	8 0	1040	..	..	..	..

Sundays

	mrn L		aft L		aft L		aft L
80 MANCHESTER (Cen.) dep	..	..	1215	..	..	..	..
77 " (Lon. Rd.) "	6 50	..	..	..	5 50	..	7 45
Guide Bridge dep	7 49	..	1239	..	6 39	..	8 37
Dukinfield	..	..	..	..	..	..	..
Ashton (Park Parade)	7 53	..	1243	..	6 43	..	8 41
Stalybridge arr	7 58	..	1248	..	6 48	..	8 46

Week Days

Miles		mrn	mrn	mrn	mrn	mrn		aft S	aft S	aft S	aft S		aft	aft S	aft E		aft E	aft E		aft	aft S			
—	Stalybridge dep	7 6	7 52	8 12	8 44	9 25	..	1214	1250	1 40	2 11	..	4 0	5 10	5 10	..	5 45	6 32	..	8 25	11 0	..	..	..
1¼	Ashton (Park Parade)	7 10	7 58	8 16	8 48	9 28	..	1217	1253	1 43	2 14	..	4 3	5 13	5 13	..	5 48	6 35	..	8 28	..	..	..	..
1¾	Dukinfield	7 13	8 1	8 18	8 50	9 30	..	1219	1255	1 45	2 16	..	4 5	5 15	5 15	..	5 50	6 37	..	8 31	..	..	..	..
2½	Guide Bridge arr	7 15	8 3	8 20	8 53	9 32	..	1221	1258	1 48	2 19	..	4 7	5 18	5 18	..	5 53	6 39	..	8 33	11 7	..	..	..
7½	77 MANCHESTER (L. Rd.) arr	7 34	8 21	8 41	9 10	1025	..	1240	1 12	2 22	2 36	..	4 25	5 35	5 42	..	6 12	6 53	..	8 53	1124	..	..	..
13¼	80 " (Central) "	8 3	8 40	9 16	..	9 57	..	1 7	..	2 29	..	..	..	..	5 59	..	6 30	7 19	..	..	..	..	..	..

Sundays

	mrn L		aft L		aft L		
Stalybridge dep	8 50	..	1 55	..	7 15	..	..
Ashton (Park Parade)	8 53	..	1 58	..	7 18	..	..
Dukinfield	..	..	..	..	..	..	..
Guide Bridge arr	8 57	..	2 2	..	7 22	..	..
77 MANCHESTER (L. Rd.) arr	9 29	..	2 41	..	..	..	..
80 " (Central) "	..	..	..	..	..	..	..

A Through train between Manchester (Cen.) and Stalybridge. E Except Sats. L L.M.S. Train between Guide Bridge and Stalybridge. S or S Sats. only.

Table 76

GUIDE BRIDGE, ASHTON, and OLDHAM

Week Days

Miles		mn	mrn	mrn	mrn L	mrn	mrn L	mrn L	mrn	mrn S	mrn E		aft S L	aft E	aft S	aft L	aft S L	aft S L	aft S	aft L	aft	aft L	aft S	aft E L	aft S L	aft	aft E L	aft E L	aft	aft L	aft S L	aft
	77 MANCHESTER (L.Rd.) dep	..	6 5	6 58	..	8 24	..	..	10 5	1058	11 8	..	..	1212	1227	..	..	..	1 40	..	2 40	..	4 20	..	..	5 20	..	..	6 31	..	..	7 25
—	Guide Bridge dep	515	6 30	7 19	..	8 50	..	..	1026	1141	1141	..	..	1244	1244	..	..	..	2 27	..	3 8	..	4 49	..	..	5 42	..	..	6 49	..	..	7 57
1¾	Ashton (Oldham Road)	522	6 35	7 24	8 19	8 55	9 2	10 5	1031	1146	1146	..	1220	1249	1249	1 9	1 36	2 3	2 32	2 47	3 13	3 35	4 54	5 6	5 34	5 48	6 14	6 28	6 55	7 12	7 30	8 2
3½	Park Bridge	528	6 40	7 29	8 24	9 0	9 7	1011	1036	1151	1151	..	1225	1255	1255	1 14	1 42	2 9	2 37	2 53	3 18	3 40	4 59	5 12	5 40	5 53	6 19	6 33	7 0	..	7 36	8 7
5¼	Oldham (Clegg Street)	533	6 45	7 34	8 29	9 5	9 12	1016	1042	1156	1156	..	1229	1 0	1 0	1 19	1 47	2 13	2 42	2 58	3T28	3 45	5 5	5 17	5 45	5 58	6 24	6 38	7 5	7 21	7 42	8 12
5¾	" (Glodwick Road) arr	535	6 47	7 36	8 34	9 12	9 15	1023	1041	1158	1158	..	1233	1 2	1 2	1S37	1 50	2N16	..	3 1	3 30	..	5 7	5 24	5 49	6 0	6 26	6 42	7 12	7 32	7 47	8 14

Week Days—Continued

	aft S L	aft E L	aft S	aft E L	aft S L	aft	aft E L	aft S L	aft S	aft S	
77 MANCHESTER (L.Rd.) dep	..	..	7 58	..	..	9 25	..	..	1030	1058	..
Guide Bridge dep	..	..	9 0	..	..	9 52	..	..	1052	1121	..
Ashton (Oldham Road)	8 29	8 33	9 5	9 19	9 42	9 57	10 8	10 26	1056	1125	..
Park Bridge	8 35	8 39	9 10	9 25	9 48	10 2	10 15	10 31	11 1	1130	..
Oldham (Clegg Street)	8 40	8 44	9 15	9 30	9 53	10 7	10 20	10 36	11 6	1136	..
" (Glodwick Road) arr	8 52	8 52	9 22	9 35	10 2	1011	10N23	10N38	11 8	1138	..

Sundays

	mrn	mrn	mrn L	mrn	mrn		aft	aft	aft L	aft		aft	aft L	aft	aft	aft L	Commences 28th May	aft	aft L	aft
77 MANCHESTER (L.Rd.) dep	8 28	9 10	..	1030	..	..	1215	..	..	3 35	..	4 50	..	5 50	6 50	..		8 40	..	1015
Guide Bridge dep	8 46	9 38	..	1051	1130	..	12 40	1 29	..	4 5	..	5 12	..	6 12	7 12	..		9 12	..	1032
Ashton (Oldham Road)	8 51	9 43	10 7	1056	..	..	12 45	1 34	2 9	4 10	..	5 17	5 30	6 17	7 17	8 51		9 17	1020	1037
Park Bridge	..	..	..	..	..	..	..	..	..	..	..	..	..	..	..	..		..	..	..
Oldham (Clegg Street)	9 0	9 55	1015	11 5	1142	..	12 54	1 43	2 17	4 19	..	5 26	5 38	6 26	7 26	8 59		9 26	1028	1046
" (Glodwick Road) arr	9 2	9 58	1032	11 7	..	..	12 56	1 45	2 22	4 21	..	5 28	6 17	6 28	7 28	9 1		9 28	1034	..

Week Days

Miles		mrn	mrn L	mrn	mrn L	mrn L	mrn	mrn L	mrn L	mrn	mrn	mrn S L	mrn L	aft	aft S L	aft L	aft S L	aft	aft L	aft S	aft L		aft S	aft E	aft L	aft S	aft E L	aft	aft L	aft S L	aft	aft L
—	Oldham (Glodwick Road) dep	5 50	6 50	6 57	7 19	7 54	8 3	8 33	9N5	..	1054	1125	1125	12 4	1238	1 24	1N36	1 54	2 0	2 26	3 30	..	4 20	4 25	4 31	5 11	5 30	6 5	6 28	6 55	7 5	8 14
½	" (Clegg Street)	5 52	6 53	6 59	7 28	7 59	8 6	8 36	9 12	9 17	1059	1130	1142	12 7	1241	1 27	1 39	1 56	2 3	2 50	3 34	..	4 22	4 30	4 38	5 13	5 34	6 9	6 32	7 5	7 17	8 19
2¼	Park Bridge	5 57	6 58	7 4	7 32	..	8 11	8 41	..	9 22	11 3	1135	..	1212	1245	1 31	..	2 1	2 7	..	3 38	..	4 27	4 34	4 42	5 18	5 38	6 14	6 37	7 10	7 22	8 23
4	Ashton (Oldham Road)	6 2	7 3	7 9	7 36	8 6	8 15	8 45	9 19	9 26	11 7	1139	1149	1216	1249	1 35	1 46	2 6	2 11	2 56	3 42	..	4 32	4 38	4 46	5 23	5 42	6 19	6 41	7 15	7 26	8 28
5¾	Guide Bridge arr	6 7	..	7 13	..	..	8 20	..	..	9 31	1112	..	..	1220	..	..	..	2 11	..	3 1	..	..	4 37	4 43	..	5 28	..	6 24	..	..	7 31	..
10¾	77 MANCHESTER (L. Rd.) arr	6 25	..	7 34	..	..	8 41	..	..	9D57	1141	..	..	12B51	..	..	..	2‡38	..	3 17	..	..	4 57	5 12	..	5 48	..	6 44	..	..	7 48	..

Week Days—Cont.

	aft S	aft E	aft S	aft L	aft	aft S
Oldham (Glodwick Road) dep	8 29	8 48	9 16	9 50	1022	1115
" (Clegg Street)	8 32	8 51	9 23	9 56	1024	1118
Park Bridge	8 37	8 56	9 28	10 1	1029	1123
Ashton (Oldham Road)	8 41	9 0	9 33	10 6	1034	1128
Guide Bridge arr	8 46	9 5	9 38	..	1039	1133
77 MANCHESTER (L. Rd.) arr	9 11	9 34	10 4	..	11F8	..

Sundays

	mrn L	mrn	mrn	mrn L	mrn	aft	aft L	aft	aft	Thro' Train, Oldham (C. St.) to Glossop (Table 67a)	aft L	aft	aft	aft L	aft	aft	aft	aft L
Oldham (Glodwick Road) dep	8 35	9 6	10 8	..	1110	..	1218	1 5	1 50		3 35	4 28	5 43	5 58	6 33	7 35	9 40	10 9
" (Clegg Street)	8 37	9 8	1010	1027	1112	12 5	1240	1 7	1 53		3 47	4 30	5 45	6 15	6 35	7 37	9 42	1014
Park Bridge	..	..	..	..	..	..	..	..	..		..	..	..	..	..	..	..	..
Ashton (Oldham Road)	8 46	9 16	1018	1035	1121	1214	1248	1 16	2 1		3 55	4 39	5 54	6 23	6 44	7 46	9 51	1022
Guide Bridge arr	..	9 20	1022	..	1125	1219	..	1 20	2 5		..	4 43	5 58	..	6 48	7 51	9 55	..
77 MANCHESTER (L. Rd.) arr	..	..	1057	..	1159	..	..	1 53	2 41		..	5 0	6 23	..	7 25	8 40	1010	..

B Arr. 12 40 aft on Sats.
D Manchester (Central)
E Except Saturdays
F Arr. 11 4 aft on Saturdays
‡ Arr. 2 29 aft on Saturdays
L L.M.S. Train
N Oldham (Mumps) Station
S or S Saturdays only
T Arr. 3 28 aft

apparent. I should add too that there was no sign of any form of central heating, instead every room except those formed by the aforementioned corridor had a fireplace, and in every fireplace was a very welcoming fire.

I was told later by some of the ladies I met this first morning that I looked sufficiently ill to appear on the point of collapse, but I felt only too delighted that I really was in a transport atmosphere, and a London & North Eastern one at that, so I tried to take in all that I was told. Needless to say when I came to leave Gorton there was no suitable train from Guide Bridge back to Oldham, so I had to take a trolleybus from the end of Cornwall Street to Ashton-under-Lyne and a motor bus on the Rochdale service from there to my destination.

I started work some 10 days later, now catching the 8.06 am from Oldham Clegg Street to Guide Bridge and the 8.32 am from there to Gorton. This train was invariably 'C13'-hauled but there was a morning 'spotting' bonus in the form of the 8.20 am from Manchester London Road to Sheffield due to depart from Guide Bridge at the same time. This usually dashed in just before my train from Hadfield put in an appearance and it was certainly worth noting. A London express in pre-war days, it now, after a 40 minute rest in Sheffield, travelled only to Doncaster and the motive power seldom consisted of the same class of engine that had worked it the previous day. Great Central Atlantics, 'Directors', every variety of 4-6-0, 'Footballers', the odd North Eastern type, Great Northern Atlantics, and even on one occasion a 'J39' 0-6-0, passed before my eyes over the next 12 months, by which time I had come to know several of the drivers in the particular link. They, if working on an engine with right-hand drive, would when seeing me on the down platform give a cheery wave.

On arrival at the office Fred Kemp took me in hand and explained to me its various mysteries the biggest of which centred around the telephone system and the so called telephone room, housing three different instruments of very different form. The 'room' itself formed a continuation of the chief clerk's office and so was in turn a continuation of that corridor. Thus having no heating at all it promoted in winter 'high speed conversation'. On the table by the window stood the GPO candlestick telephone (East 0649). This was always referred to as 'The National' presumably because before 1912 when the National Telephone Company was taken over by the GPO, the Great Central Railway was connected to that system. Tradition died hard at Gorton. This we were not encouraged to use if there was an alternative as a GPO call cost the company money so let us turn to the remaining alternatives.

The second phone, wall-mounted was of the 'Wild West' variety. You vigorously rotated the handle that sprouted from its side, and eventually the operator would respond, and ask what number or place you were calling. This phone linked other offices across Cornwall Street, and the workshop offices, the operator herself being located somewhere so well buried in the 'Tank' that I never did know where that switchboard actually was. Now this system was reasonably reliable, and more or less audible, but number three was a very different affair altogether.

It was based on a large slab of best mahogany around 2 ft in depth, and say 18 inches wide. At the top were several bells, and below them about eight horizontally mounted bobbins with labels beneath each to provide the requisite

The Guide Bridge push-and-pull train approaches Oldham on the climb from Park Bridge. The leading coach is the former first class vehicle that suffered a broken window when my feet slipped on that wet compartment floor.

Guide Bridge station, now largely demolished, was where I changed twice each day. 'C13' class 4-4-2T No. 67447 stands at the up main platform. No buildings now exist on it nor on the one serving the down main line opposite. The subway too no longer exists. The coach is one of Dukinfield carriage and wagon works' later products forming half of an articulated set.

identification. Below these again was a box, standing out from the base by some six inches, and mounted on this was the father or mother of all subsequent microphones. Nearby was a white bell push, and from the box sprouted two flexible tubes with what appeared to be ivory earpieces on the ends thereof. These tubes were normally housed in rests mounted on either side of the box. Finally to complete this piece of medieval apparatus was a sort of small brass poker that hung from the board on a chain of the same material. Now all one had to do was to make the desired call, but before you could do that a detailed knowledge of circuit geography was essential when good luck thereafter became a prerequisite.

To ring say the wet pit or to give it the proper title 'Running Foreman Cabin No. 2', one inserted the poker in the centre of the bobbin marked 'yard circuit'. Then you placed the tubes to each ear and listened. Was anyone else speaking on that circuit? No, then press the appropriate bell code, in this case two pause one. Every telephone bell on every instrument on that circuit would then give out that message, but if you failed to see if the circuit was in use before pressing that act would blot out the associated conversations - something that was not going to make you very popular. Now luck came into the equation for you needed someone not only to be there in the wet pit cabin but also to recognise your two pause one signal as being for him, and then do something about it by lifting off his ear tubes, and speaking into his microphone. As the wet pit was only a mile or so away, it was possible to hear the voice coming from that end of the line reasonably well, but what of a long distance call?

I was given the task one day of trying to locate one of our locomotives that was as it were 'absent without leave', and this involved putting in a call to Cambridge. One started the process by plugging into the London Road circuit, and telling the operator there exactly what you wanted. She would then book your call and with luck a day or two later our telephone attendant would begin to walk round the offices calling out 'Call to Cambridge in'. It could and did take that long, but whether the delay was due to the volume of traffic or the lack of phone lines over Woodhead, was something I never did discover. Oft times all the effort was wasted as one had either forgotten about placing the call in the first place, or had solved the problem by other means or, whisper it darkly, had resorted in desperation to the National. But if speech was still called for via the 'Thing' then up came another snag. Voltage drop must have been enormous, as you just could not make out what the Cambridge contact was saying so some other kind operator down the line, perhaps at Lincoln, would have to act as an intermediary, and relay what was being said in both directions to the parties to the call. One did not use this remarkable innovation (well it was at the turn of the century) without careful thought.

Now it might be said that centralising a telephone system has some advantages, but in this case any such benefits were far from obvious. True the lack of heating in the phone room did tend to cut things short in winter time, but when three people were endeavouring to engage in three conversations simultaneously, in a small and echoing room and one of those is trying to make themselves heard to a person east of Sheffield the chances of profound misunderstandings occurring were endless.

My first job was to write out blue company free invoices for the many wagons of ash lifted each day from the wet pit, these wagons being dispatched to places decided by the district engineer, who was located in the upper floors of Guide Bridge station building. For some weeks wagon movements went without a hitch, but then came a dearth of disposal instructions, and wagons began to fill, and overfill, the available wet pit siding space. The wet pit foreman rang the invoice writer and engaged in a process known as 'Ear bending', so I did the obvious. I rang Guide Bridge, and asked to speak to the district engineer then a Mr Lees. He came on the line, I explained the situation, and he obviously not realising he was speaking to a very junior 16-years-old clerk promised to look into things for me.

He was as good as his word, and the following morning the telephone attendant came into our office to call 'National telephone call for Geoffrey'. Now it so chanced that Mr Sayers was close by at the time, when he stopped me in my tracks, and in brisk tones began to make it very clear that private phone calls were *not* permitted. Now the lady broke in to say it was not a private call, it was in fact no less a person than the Guide Bridge district engineer in person. My chief clerk seemed somewhat bemused by this piece of information, so he told me to hurry up, and not keep such an exalted officer waiting.

Two minutes later the wagon problem was solved, all were to be invoiced to the then new Dean Shutt sidings which were located on the Oldham side of Park Bridge station, so I thanked him for his assistance, and left to face an interrogation as to why Mr Lees had asked for me in person. I was beginning to think that trouble was heading my way, but Mr Rowbottom who had heard all that had transpired and seemed rather amused by the outcome entered the conversation and suggested to Mr Sayers that I had used my initiative. So our chief departed for his room and the matter was allowed to rest, but although I did not know it, my days of writing out blue free invoices were almost at an end and this incident might just have had something to do with what followed.

Of the staff in the general section Messrs Rowbottom and Gregory obviously took care of the more important work that came in, whilst Mr Hockram looked after district coal supplies and matters appertaining thereto. Mr and Mrs Clappison covered engine allocations and the all important availability return. This document covered every district shed having the days of the week across the top and a list of every engine allocated to each shed set down vertically. If one worked or was available for work an 'A' was entered in the appropriate square, if not some other reason was marked in, e.g. 'WO' for washout. This was an exercise that kept them busy and considerable telephone users. Fred Kemp dealt with the then important ARP matters plus a variety of miscellaneous tasks, whilst Miss Ennever covered train delays and engine failures. She then gave in her notice, and I came to inherit her work but I have no doubt that but for wartime conditions no 16-year-old junior would have been doing that job.

Letters would come in from the district superintendent, now evacuated to Godley (phone Hyde 971), from Mr Leedham Manager of the Cheshire Lines Committee (CLC) or from other similar sources, and could well be worded as follows:

9.45 am Manchester to London. 17th May, 1943.

The above train was delayed 17 minutes awaiting entry to Penistone station due to the up platform road being occupied by the 5.30 am Guide Bridge North to Wath, which stood in the station for some 25 minutes. As this train was headed by a Gorton engine I would be obliged to know the reason for this unwarranted delay.

per A R Dunbar
District Superintendent

If this was the first intimation of any such occurrence I would open the 'T' book at the due dated page and write in the heading 5.30 am Guide Bridge North etc. giving the affair the next available 'T' reference number. Now it might be that later in the day a driver's report form would come in, but if not I had to hunt for the relevant driver's work ticket. These were quite large white forms that were filled in on the front by that individual and then handed to the guard who inserted on the back running details of the train or trains worked and which showed any time booked against the locomotive in the process. These tickets went through the Locomotive Accountant's offices which were across Cornwall Street. In those pre-computer days a bevy of young ladies punched out cards for the Hollerith system to provide engine mileage and other relevant statistics, so a visit to those offices and a diplomatic request to have access to piles of tickets then being worked on was essential. One had to be careful not to mix them up in such circumstances or when looking for ones that had been processed for these were placed in cupboards lining the walls of the chief mechanical engineer's office corridor. This was worthy of detailed study, for on the walls above those cupboards were numerous quite large framed photographs of Gorton locomotives many bearing the bold autographed inscription 'John G. Robinson'.

This, though, was the easy part, for our district locomotive superintendent, then Mr C.B. Kirk, was also responsible for the locomotives stationed at Wigan (Mr Ball), Trafford Park (Mr Darley), Stockport (Mr Foster), Walton (Mr Dobson), Brunswick (Mr Hellowell), Northwich (Mr Hewitt), Chester, Bidston (Mr Ottaway) and Wrexham (Mr Lawler) together with the much smaller establishments at Hayfield and Dinting where a chargehand driver held sway. It was those western places in the main that were the brunt of Mr Leedham's complaints only one had to have some sympathy for the management of the CLC as so many of its trains were hauled by engines of classes such as 'J10', 'N5', 'F1', 'F2', 'N5', 'D6' and 'D10', most of which even by 1942/3 standards were decidedly long in the proverbial tooth. I would therefore draft out letters to the gentlemen at these sheds asking for their comments on problems caused by their charges. When prompt replies were not always forthcoming I then resorted to 'repeating'. Being wartime and printed paper being in short supply someone in the LNER had devised a small but very nifty form. You filled in the various heading details and then inserted a number against the words 'Clause number applies'. At the left-hand side of this form were a series of numbers carried on also overleaf, and against each number was a printed sentence, that by clause No. 7 if I remember rightly saying, 'Please let me have a reply to my letter of . . !' I would add in the date, apply a stamp at the foot saying 'C.B. Kirk

Gorton station as it was. One arrived on the down main (*left*) platform and crossed the footbridge. The path to the top office ran between the school hall and the top of the embankment towards the rear of the train. The bag of fuel on the footplate of the locomotive is intriguing, I never recall seeing anything similar in my Gorton days.

From time to time a friendly driver, knowing I worked in the Top Office, would let me ride with him on the footplate from Guide Bridge to Oldham when with a working push-and-pull set the engine always led. A 'C13' tank was the usual motive power, but 'F1' class 2-4-2 tank No. 5594 was also fitted up for this type of work and being allocated to Gorton appeared in my earliest days. Into the 1930s the 'F1' class worked many of the Manchester suburban services, No. 5576 being a typical example. They did good work, the last two examples of the 39 built from 1889 surviving until 1949.

per district locomotive superintendent' and pass the pile, some days as many as 40 forms at a time, to Mr Sayer for him to initial; he might if busy might pass them back to me for my best attempt at forgery.

There were two very serious documents to complete, initially in draft to the best of my ability. The first was a casualty return to be sent to the locomotive running superintendent (Mr G.A. Musgrave) at Gerrards Cross, outlining the circumstances whenever a locomotive failed in traffic, but here we were in deep technicalities and so the assistant district locomotive superintendent had to be asked to verify what was written and then add his signature to the form, and here I come to mention Mr J.F. Ivors. A nephew of John G. Robinson, Mr Ivors was then middle-aged, an Irishman, a character, and universally respected. It was stoutly maintained that amongst his other readily repeated pronouncements was one where, after taking two late-reporting fire watchers to task, he sternly added, 'And next time you had better be on duty 10 minutes before the sirens sound'. He was, though, very good humoured and sadly, profoundly deaf, and here lay another seed for tragedy. I would fill in as much of the form as I could and then await his coming when I would, for example, ask, 'How did the gudgeon pin on a "J39" come to work out?' He would attempt to give me an explanation, but being deaf he spoke in a very loud voice so every one else in the office received the benefit of his response, but more of this later.

The other document was the monthly train delay form that also found its way to Gerrards Cross. At the requisite time I would make up a draft list of every passenger train in our district that was delayed by (I think) more than 10 minutes as a result of some engine problem. This I then presented to Mr Rowbottom for his inspection, when some editing became the order of the day before it went before the district locomotive superintendent for his final approval. Could one safely assume that, Woodhead being a long way from Gerrards Cross, 'engine slipping greasy rail' might be set down instead of 'sands completely inoperative' as recorded by the driver, or would 'strong sidewind' be acceptable in those kinder Buckinghamshire climes, when some ailing Gorton 'B17' class simply refused to make steam.

Now Mr Rowbottom was a kindly man whom I remember with affection, but he had a peculiarity of his own, and that was a decided anti dust and dirt phobia. All the office windows were sealed which was perhaps just as well as looking through those windows one's eyes alighted on the sponge cloth laundry. This was presided over by Head Office inspector Earsden whose office was a partitioned off section in the corridor to the left of the main entrance door, only his chargehand Dick Bray seemed to do most of the work involved. The laundry was a gem as here the oil was extracted from used cleaning wipes, and put into barrels for the lubrication of point rodding, etc. I visited the premises on about two occasions and that was quite enough. It was far from anything a present day Health & Safety Inspector would pass, but even so it was worth seeing - once!

This phobia which called for frequent visits to the washroom also came to the fore if I had to look out some previously filed paperwork for him. We did not have an indexed filing system, letters were stored in cardboard folders or pads kept on open shelves in various parts of the office. Here they gathered dust so *never* was I allowed to deposit such a pad on his desk. Mine yes after dusting, his never, but he was kind to me and so readily agreed one early day to Fred's suggestion that I might go with him on one of his fairly frequent trips to the shed.

Consequently for the first time I walked down the works yard, past the end of the foundry, over the tracks leading to the new boiler shop and other adjacent buildings with their old boiler plate roadway surfacing, under the famous bird cage footbridge, and down the cobbled path to the buildings fronting on to Wellington Street. Here I met Mr Cooper the list clerk, was shown the office Mr Ivors used and then was introduced to Mr Carter the store keeper whose written communications were often penned not only in various forms of script, but also in multi-coloured hues of ink, he was another character!

Then we walked along the path to the side door way to the shed and there under the roof in front of me was the breakdown train with its replacement steam crane. I believe this came from Woodford after the original was commandeered for war service and lost at sea when *en route* to the Middle East. We then reached the shed office where I met Mr Maugham, the long serving and well respected ex-GCR shed foreman, and one or two of the other staff members. Fred took me for a walk round and I came to the conclusion very quickly that the pen was mightier than the spanner and the top office a much more pleasant place of employment, little thinking what the later years would bring. Then we arrived at a 'B17' class 4-6-0 being prepared for a run to Sheffield. We climbed to the footplate, Fred spoke to the driver and I had a chat with the fireman who began to show me what all the handles or wheels did. The driver remarked, 'Young one seems interested' when Fred said, 'He is, you will have to take him for a trip'. I could not believe my ears but Dick Ball, a long standing Gorton top link driver, agreed and we began to discuss when.

Now it so happened that on Saturday night next my parents and I were due to travel to Newcastle-upon-Tyne to visit relatives there. On that same night Mr Ball was due to work the 5.27 pm from Manchester Central to Sheffield, this being the late afternoon Liverpool to Hull through train. So all I had to do was to persuade the folks that the direct route from Manchester to our destination lay via Sheffield and Doncaster and *not* via Huddersfield and Leeds. Fortunately there seemed to be a good connection north from Doncaster, so at around 5.00 pm on the 28th August we stood on Central station and watched the train come in on time from Liverpool behind the usual 'D9' class 4-4-0. The Gorton 'B17' then backed onto what had been the rear end, and Dick Ball climbed down from the footplate of No. 2871 *Manchester City* to dash my feelings of anticipation. It was a typical Manchester summer evening, grey, misty, and drizzling, so after looking over light coloured flannels and sports coat Dick indicated that they were not quite the thing to wear for a trip through Woodhead tunnel, but he had promised me a ride, so I could come aboard at Penistone. We left as scheduled at 5.27 pm, but lost time to Guide Bridge, and a good deal more to Woodhead, but at last Penistone was reached and I did a dash forward to be greeted by Dick and his fireman Sidney Rickards. The latter wiped the top of the 'piano' stool on his side of the cab, bade me sit down, and then coming behind me said, 'This is a rough old crate, but don't be frightened, just hold on'. The cheek I thought, me scared never.

As he finished speaking Dick opened the regulator, No. 2871 gave a lurch, and we began to move and as we did that locomotive began to 'dance'. The cab floor lifted and fell, only to repeat the process whilst at the same time a side to side motion ensued. Then as the floor went one way, the cab and boiler appeared to go another, and all this was accompanied by noise, a sort of very loud thumping from below. By Barnsley Junction I just wanted to get off, but we were late, so Dick opened the regulator further, when all the previous sensations were alarmingly magnified. I was appalled, never had I imagined that a fast train footplate ride would be as wild as this.

The most terrifying part was as we shot round a curve at Thurgoland when No. 2871 seemed to climb the rails and when a loud crash came from beneath. During all this Sidney stood behind me and explained items of interest, only I am sorry to say that I was too shattered to comprehend.

At last we ground to a halt in Sheffield Victoria. I tottered out my thanks, and climbed down from the cab, nearly fell over once on the platform, and gained our compartment to be greeted by mother's comments on my clothes and appearance. Worse though was to come.

Leaving Sheffield about 45 minutes late, we missed our connection at Doncaster, not reaching Newcastle until the early hours of Sunday morning, by which time the parents were certainly not LNER fans. I was told in no uncertain terms that our journey home would be via a through train from Newcastle to Manchester. After experiencing *Manchester City* my appetite for footplate riding was considerably diminished, and truth to tell, I rather supported the decision. If No. 2871 was a fair 'B17' example, then no wonder Gorton men had little good to say about the class of 'Footballers' in general. As I came to find out later - it was!

My next footplate trip was very different. I had asked if I might be allowed to visit all the sheds in our district, and the answer came back in the affirmative, provided that I did so in my own time, when I had not to interfere in any way with their various workings. So one warm Saturday afternoon I took a train from Manchester Central to Wigan Central, and then made my way to the ex-GCR shed at Lower Ince. I was intrigued in the process by Wigan station which was obviously unfinished, wondering as I gazed at the structure what things would have been like if the proposed extensions to meet the West Lancashire Railway near Preston, and the further extension thence to Blackpool, had ever been constructed. I soon found my way to the shed, but alas there was not a lot to see. However, my disappointment here was offset quickly by the person in sole charge that afternoon. Wigan then had an allocation of around ten 'J10s' and a solitary 'J11' which was obviously the pride of the stud. This machine was at home that afternoon, so I was escorted onto the footplate, and we spent a happy hour shuttling up and down the shed tracks whilst I was given a course of driving instruction. When that came to an end I boarded the footplate of a 'J10' heading tender first to the station, and then had a trip on it as far as Glazebrook.

After that I visited every one of our depots with the exception of Walton and began to wonder just how some of them managed to function. For example Brunswick was so cramped as to be congestion unlimited, whilst Bidston

Seventy-three 'B17' class 4-6-0 locomotives, Nos. 2800-2872 were built between 1928 and 1936, Gorton getting its first, No. 2802, new to work the through Liverpool to Harwich train which it powered through from Manchester (Central) to Ipswich. No. 2802 was from the 2800-2847 series - the 'Sandringhams' - with small Great Eastern-type tender, a second was allocated in 1931, then a third. Later the 'Footballers', Nos. 2848 to 2872, were built with group standard larger tenders and by 1937 seven of these were on Gorton's allocation - they were far from popular. Most had left by 1939 but several reappeared in 1942 to bring the number up to eight. I rode on some of them and I can only say that No. 2871 *Manchester City* was a fair sample. They also came into works for overhaul until 1944 and I recall seeing the last in two bay still in green livery. No one was sorry to see them leave but this was only temporary, Gorton Shed finally lost its last 'B17s' in 1946. The best part of these locomotives was the boiler which, as type '100A', was modified by Edward Thompson and fitted to 'B1s', 'O1s' and 'O4/8s'. In this view No. 2871 *Manchester City* is captured by the photographer at Nottingham (Victoria) with the 2.20 pm Manchester (London Road)-Marylebone on 7th August, 1937.   *T.G. Hepburn/Rail Archive Stephenson*

The first 'B1' class, No. 8301 *Springbok*, was turned out from Darlington in December 1942, another 409 appearing later. It came to Gorton in March 1943 and then ran trials against a home 'B17' class. Later No. 8307 joined it but by the end of 1944 both had moved on. No. 8301 was renumbered as 1000 in early 1946 and was withdrawn in March 1962.

seemed wild and windswept even on a summer day. Trafford Park was really half a shed thanks to a large area of missing roof, but contained a spotting bonus in the shape of three of the CLC Sentinel railcars that seemed to have been laid up for quite a time.

Whilst this tour was under way Dick Ball said I could have a ride with him one night on the 10.40 pm from Sheffield so to that city I repaired. The engine working the train was a 'K3' class fortunately fresh from overhaul, so the riding quality was far better than that of No. 2871, and as we were heading downhill through Woodhead tunnel I found my first trip through it to be a lot less troublesome than I had been warned to expect. This train then stopped at Gorton, so I left the footplate there and headed for the enginemen's barracks where I had a bed for the night, and so was in good time to start work in the office the following morning. Here I must digress and comment on the subject of office time keeping. My last task each evening was to lay out on my desk a pen, a bottle of red ink, a ruler and the signature book.

The following morning as staff arrived they would 'sign in' but at a few minutes before nine Mr Sayer would appear and stand with his back to the firegrate. As the hour struck he would step forward with majestic tread, and draw a red line under the last signature. When the next person dashed in and as they placed their name below that telling line, our chief clerk would take his gold watch from his waistcoat pocket, snap it open, compare its time with that of the office clock, and cough ominously. At five past the hour he would pick up the book and march with it into his office. If you came in thereafter you had to give a full account as to why you were not present by nine o'clock.

Additionally, wartime or not, we had to appear in the office suitably dressed, a suit, collar and tie being essential and of course we had to be present for work every Saturday morning. But on reflection now I cannot help thinking that standards have slipped rather too far, and a general lack of respect for authority is a cause of many of our present problems. One of my problems, though, was having to learn to type and do shorthand so that by 18-years-of-age I would be able to meet the company's proficiency standards if my position was to become permanent. This entailed attending our local commercial college three nights a week finding myself the only boy in a class of 14 girls, but here there were definite compensations, as I was rather better at commercial arithmetic than they were so I was never short of either sweets or dancing partners, life on the whole was decidedly pleasant.

It improved some more when the first 'B1' class 4-6-0 No. 8301 *Springbok* arrived at Gorton for trials against a home-based 'B17' whose number I have now forgotten. The engines worked through to or from London during this period and the ebullient inspector Tommy Adams rode on the footplates taking note of passing times, boiler and steam chest pressure and cut off. One of the more senior clerks turned the first collection of data into a series of graphs, and then the task of producing the ensuing examples was handed to me, the shed joiner making up an illuminated tracing table for the purpose. When the tests were over *Springbok* began to work other trains and needless to say driver Richard Ball soon found his hand on the regulator. So one night I had a trip on the 3.30 pm from Marylebone which left Sheffield at 8.05 pm and as there was

Gorton's largest express locomotives, the six 'B3s' (GCR '9P') and their 38 'B7' ('9Q') cousins had several unusual features. The outside cylinders drove onto the centre axle and to keep equal length connecting rods the slide bars were not fixed to the cylinders but to the substantial castings bolted to the frames as shown here. Note also how the very long piston rod passed through these same castings. To try to improve the rather disappointing 'B3' performance four of them were given Caprotti gear, two in 1929, the others with a modified version in 1938 and 1939. Their cam boxes were not covered to improve their cooling after earlier complete enclosure.

The first of the 'K3s' were built for the Great Northern Railway in 1920/21 at Doncaster, being numbered 1000 to 1009 - later 4000 to 4009 in the LNER series - 173 more examples followed to 1937. Gorton works never saw them but Gorton Shed did - witness the saga of No. 4001. Powerful mixed traffic engines when 'on song' they quickly gained a reputation for rough riding. I was on a typical example one day on the Rotherham to Sheffield line which suddenly gave a vicious lurch. A mighty grab for a handrail followed as I had visions of being decanted into the River Don. The driver simply grinned and said 'Tha's not got thy sea legs yet then?' Pictured below is 'K3' No. 2440 at Nottingham Victoria on 31st July, 1938.

T.G. Hepburn/Rail Archive Stephenson

a connection off this service at Guide Bridge for Oldham there was no need for me to spend the night at Gorton. As Dick said, No. 8301 rode 'like a private car' and now one could sit in some comfort, not on a piano stool, but on a proper upholstered seat.

It was sad when our hours in the afternoon were lengthened as I had to travel home most nights by bus, but kindly Miss Fisher in the staff section eased my lot here by suggesting to Mr Rowbottom that it would be helpful if I could leave early for Guide Bridge, in order to leave the staff at the booking on point there sundry packets of bus tokens and obtain a signature for them on the spot, so there could be no chance of error. To this suggestion my section chief assented without the slightest demur.

Other people also were making kindly suggestions to me. If you came through that door in the wall and turned left, you passed Mr Earsdon's partitioned-off base and so came to the big office fronting Cornwall Street where our three locomotive inspectors did their paper work; Messrs Howard of pre-war Continental fame, Tommy Adams later to be Lord Mayor of Manchester, and firing inspector Worthington. This trio were joined about this time by Vernon Blakoe. At the far end of the room was another door leading to the lobby of the staff dining hall, which also showed every possible trace of its schooling ancestry.

One day two young men appeared and had their lunch but here was a significant difference as they were in overalls. Who and what were they? The answer was Premium Apprentices, both being the sons of fathers who to say the least held positions of some importance in the works.

It was put to me that clerking was not a job with a golden future. To be anyone in locomotive operations one needed to have technical training and so I should see if I could join what was obviously an advantageous company. But could a junior clerk make such a momentous change?

My luck held. I believe that both Mr Rowbottom and Mr Clappison spoke to Mr Ivors who broke off a discourse one morning on some casualty return (shortly after this sighting) by propelling me into the superintendent's office now Mr Bernard Atkinson B.Sc. who had replaced the retired Mr Kirk a little while previously. There he told our chief of my apparent interest and Mr Adkinson asked me a series of quite penetrating questions, but he asked some other members of the staff a whole lot more and very sorry for themselves they were too as they emerged one by one from his office on a Monday morning about this time. Previously Mr Adkinson had been superintendent at Norwich and elected one Saturday to return there for the weekend. Now Mr Ivors was aware of this fact so it was suggested to sundry shed personnel that it would be as well if the Gorton engine that was scheduled to work the 12.28 pm from London Road to Leicester was to say the least in rude health. It chanced that on shed was a 'Lord Farringdon' class 'B3' just out of the shops after overhaul, surely the obvious choice?

Alas by some mischance it was allocated to a Marple local with the result that a foreign and well rundown 'K3' class 2-6-0 No. 4001 was coupled onto the stock standing in London Road station for the 12.28 pm to Sheffield. To say that locomotive was not in the best of health was the understatement of the year. It

LONDON & NORTH EASTERN RAILWAY

L.R.S.
7522.

LOCOMOTIVE RUNNING DEPARTMENT,

SOUTHERN AREA,

GORTON STATION,

_8- 8- 1943_ DATE.

No. of Train _18_   Time due to depart _12-28_   From _LONDON Rd. to SHEFFIELD_

Actual time _____

on _SAT_ day the _8th_ day of _AUGUST_ 19_43_ Engine No. _4001_

LOAD :—Bogie Coaches _10_ 6 Wheeled _—_ Total _—_ Equal to _20_

_____ Goods _____ Coal _____ Empties, including wagons of the following carrying capacity

20 tons _____ 15 tons _____ 12 tons _____ 10 tons _____ equal to _____

Delay _38_ Minutes. At _PRIORY JUNCTION_

Delay _5_ Minutes. At _FAIRFIELD + 18 AT GUIDE BRI._

Delay _40_ Minutes. Between _GUIDE BR._ and _DUNFORD_

Delay _____ Minutes. Between _____ and _____

Delay _____ Minutes. Between _____ and _____

Time regained by Loco. _—_

State of weather _FINE_ Rail _DRY_

Cause of delay _ENGINE BADLY RUN DOWN_
GLANDS BLOWING TUBES LEAKING IN
SMOKE BOX COAL SMALL TO SLACK

Remarks _STOPPED PRIORY JNCT ETC TO RAISE_
STEAM 40 MINUTES LOST GUIDE BRIDGE
TO DUNFORD - ENGINE WOULD NOT STEAM

Fireman _F WARHURST_   SIGNED. _C. NEAVE_ Driver.

This form to be used for all delays to Passenger and Goods Trains including any late start waiting Engines.

so transpired that Uncle George's family and I were all 12.28 passengers this very day. We actually left the platform spot on time but only reached Priory Junction, a couple of miles out, when we came to a stand for our first 'blow up'. After pressure and motion had been restored we had another pause by Fairfield, and a longer one at Guide Bridge. Thereafter we had ample time to study the scenery on the Hyde Junction to Woodhead section. A copy of the driver's report has survived in my papers, and is reproduced in these pages to illustrate what was a very sorry story. Needless to say Mr Atkinson had no chance of reaching Norwich that day and repercussions followed, as on Monday a veritable procession of shed supervisors was marched in and out of his private office. This office by the way had its own national (GPO) telephone and private washing facilities so being a district locomotive superintendent had obvious advantages.

I too was scheduled for a momentous interview a few days later but this took place in a building across Cornwall Street in a large room once occupied by no less a personage than John G. Robinson himself. Now J.F. Harrison, mechanical engineer, Gorton, and once the supremo of Lower Ince, Wigan Shed sat behind the desk, and he proceed to ask me a goodly number of questions, before indicating that I should return to my own office whilst a certain request received due consideration. A second interview followed and then I was told my application had been accepted, and I was to be transferred to the works for a six months trial period. If this was satisfactory then I would be given full premium apprentice training, if not a return to my then junior clerk's status would occur, and here luck was again with me.

In earlier days a premium of £50 and been charged and no wages were paid, but as this was wartime standard apprentice rates were forthcoming and as I was already on the staff of the LNER no £50 was demanded. When in May 1963 I visited Gorton for the last time the chief staff clerk told me how well he remembered the pile of paper that resulted before the no fee decision was reached.

As a result of the foregoing, I entered up my 'T' book for the last time, had a morning off on the Saturday, purchased two pairs of overalls, and looked out some old clothes. Then on the Monday caught the familiar 8.06 am train from Oldham Clegg Street to Guide Bridge and at around 9.00 am presented myself at the offices of the locomotive works manager, which were located at the eastern end of the premises. Very soon thereafter I entered a world that was so very different from the one I had known up to that time. One last comment on my office days. The delay caused to the 9.45 am from Manchester London Road to Marylebone when it had to stand for quite a time outside Penistone station really did happen. I as usual went through the driver's tickets for the day, found the identity of the individual in charge of the offending working and sent him an appropriate inquiry. A few days later my original letter came back to me, well thumbed and nicely coal-dusted, and with the following words scrawled in blunt pencil on the reverse side 'Sir, This delay was caused by my fireman answering nature's call'. Needless to say our response to the district superintendent was of a much more technical nature.

The wartime 8.20 am from Manchester to Sheffield and Doncaster had a Gorton crew to Sheffield and if variety is the spice of life then they could never have been subject to boredom. Nearly every day saw a different class of locomotive at the head including the pioneer 1917 Gorton-built 'B3' class 4-6-0 No. 6169 *Lord Faringdon*. This was one of the two class members, the other was No. 6165 *Valour*, never to be rebuilt. Allocated to Gorton around 1943/44, No. 6169 never entered British Railways stock being withdrawn in December 1947. It is seen here at Nottingham Victoria in 1935.

Also to be seen on the 8.20 am ex-Manchester from time to time were 'C4' class Atlantics, but I was never to have a footplate trip on one until the summer of 1947. Twenty-seven of these Atlantics were built as GCR class '8B' between 1903 and 1906. No. 6093 was built by the North British Locomotive Company in 1905 and was withdrawn by British Railways in November 1948 as No. 62916.

Chapter Six

The Tank

As I was not then wearing my overalls I was able to reach the works manager's office by walking through the main door of the CME'S building, protocol was strictly applied in those days. And so I came to meet Mr H.J. Williams who then held that position. He had a short conversation with me before passing me on to his assistant Mr Simpson who was a long standing Gorton man, and very much a Great Central enthusiast, who spent considerably more time with me. Finally he detailed some junior member of his staff to conduct me to the offices of the machine shop foremen, and so I recorded another first as we walked through the boiler and plating shops to reach that destination.

I had by this time made numerous journeys to the shed, but despite each time having walked through the works yard had never realised just what lay within the outer walls that was then before my eyes The boiler and plating sections were big, dusty and very noisy, and it was the noise that struck one so forcibly. I noticed that despite all the din none of the workforce was wearing any form of ear protection, but then we came into a much loftier, and quieter, part of the premises where a surprising number of various machine tools were busy working.

The machine shop was formed of not one but two bays that had once formed part of the original works. At the eastern end of the first bay were a series of arches that had once allowed locomotives to gain access to the original erecting shop, only that area now held still more machines, the cylinder fitting section and the partitioned off brass shop. One of these bays, the western one, had until a few years earlier been provided with a gallery that had provided space for the smaller machines plus some fitting benches, this being in the period when all machines were driven by long belts and overhead shafting. Now both belts and gallery had been virtually swept away, and at least 85 per cent of all the visible equipment was obviously of very recent vintage. I came to the conclusion, after some time in the shop, that someone somewhere had come to the conclusion just prior to 1939 that with Adolf Hitler in power in Germany peace was not likely to be of long duration, and had engaged in some extensive plant renewal as a result. Such thoughts, though, were for the future. Now I found myself being introduced to Messrs Grundy and Mitchell the shop foremen, and it was the latter who took me across to the place where sat chargehand Fred Routledge, leaving me in his care with the comment, 'Give him a quiet one Fred'.

The 'quiet' one turned out to be a centring machine. This had a lathe-type bed but with a headstock at each end. Each carried a three jaw chuck, a start and stop button, and a long horizontally mounted handle. Fred picked up from an adjacent pile a forging that would eventually become the screw portion of a screw coupling. This he placed in the three jaw chuck and set it tight. Then he switched on the power, a motor drive within the headstock then turned a small

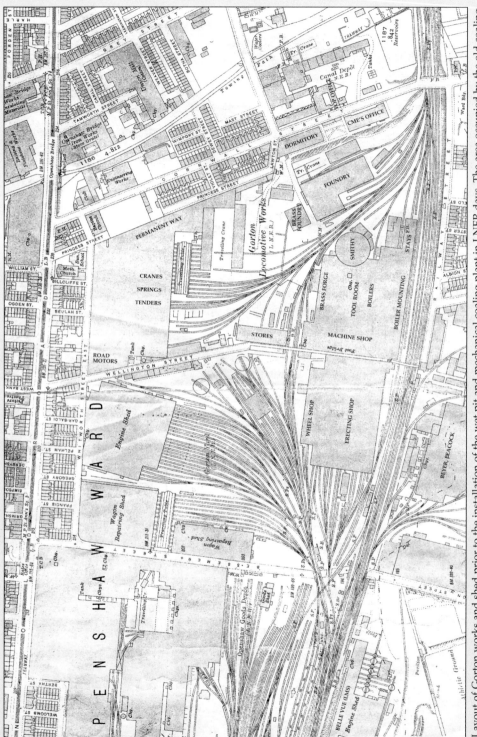

Layout of Gorton works and shed prior to the installation of the wet pit and mechanical coaling plant in LNER days. The area occupied by the old coaling stage and the lowermost turntable was later completely cleared and then used to house the new weighbridge and storage sidings.

drill located in the centre of the three jaw chuck. Pulling on the handle drew the drill forwards and so it made a hole about ⅜ in. deep in the forging, stops on the handle determining just how deep that drill could go. He then took the forging out, turned it round, and repeated the operation. Then it was my turn.

By the time the lunch break came round at 12.30 pm I had reduced that pile to minuscule proportions and was looking forward to an easier afternoon. For now standing was the order of the day, and I did rather miss the comfort of my office chair with its GC first class moquette-covered cushion. But I made my way to the staff dining room quite happily to tell my office friends as we ate our meal that 'The works didn't seem too bad'. That feeling though did not survive many minutes after 1.30 pm as on return to my machine I found that some wretch had removed all my morning's efforts and replaced them by an even larger pile of forgings. We did, however, have a tea break at 3.30 as Monday was not then an overtime day, and my day came to an end not at 5.30 pm but, by special concession, 15 minutes earlier. This early finish allowed those of the staff who needed it to catch the 5.42 pm from Guide Bridge to Oldham, which required one to reach that station on the 5.27 pm Hadfield train from Gorton station, something that was obviously impossible if one could not leave the works until half past. But obtaining this permission involved having one's foreman write out a weekly 'pass out' that could be subject to inspection as one passed through the time lodge, and here was a unique system.

You were issued with a black folding wallet which carried your number on the front in red figures, mine now being 2308. Inside the wallet reposed a time sheet, and each wallet was normally housed in its correct pigeon hole, racks of which covered both walls of the time lodge vestibule, a tunnel like structure with two big doors at either end. As you came in for a morning start, you took your wallet out of its slot, put it in your pocket, and kept it to lunch time when on the way out you threw it into a large box provided for the purpose. On returning the timekeepers would have restored it to its proper slot, whence you extracted it once more to repeat the exercise at finishing time, but what if you were late? A goodly proportion of the personnel lived not in and around Gorton, but 'up country' and so arrived at Gorton station by train using the 7.06 am from Stalybridge, the 6.45 am from Hadfield, and the 7.02 am from Marple which made a connection at that place off a Hayfield service. These three trains were timed to arrive at Gorton at 7.22, 7.30 and 7.35 respectively, in other words with sufficient time to allow the 'Tank' contingent to reach the time lodge, and their work places well before 7.55 am. Never accuse the LNER of not appreciating the facts of life.

Sometimes, but not often, these trains would run late, and then the Tank contingent would run along Lee Street down Ogden Lane, and *en masse* through those double doors where, as the time of 7.55 was reached, the timekeepers would be endeavouring to force them shut against the press, who initially at least usually won the encounter. If you lost, you waited on Cornwall Street for a few minutes, when the doors opened once more when you took out your wallet in the normal way, only to have to present it to the waiting clerk who then stamped 8.10 am on the appropriate part of your timesheet in indelible figures. Then at 8.10 the doors would close once more and the whole process

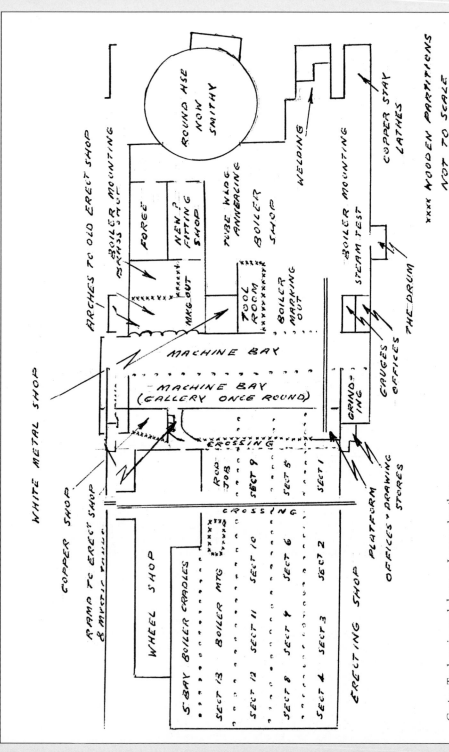

Gorton Tank main workshops as I remember them.

would be repeated only now a time sheet received a 30 minute late start endorsement. For the record we normally worked 8 hours and 35 minutes each weekday, and 4 hours 5 minutes on Saturday to reach the standard 48 hour week. On at least three nights a week many of the employees continued on overtime to 7.30 pm when the afternoon tea break was put back to 4.15 pm, but doing that overtime did make for a very long and to me a very tiring day.

I must digress and return to those morning trains. The 8.06 am from Clegg Street was now a thing of the past, I had to catch the 6.58 am which had been the second daily working from Guide Bridge, but then the 5.15 departure from that place was withdrawn so it became the first. It continued beyond Clegg Street to Glodwick Road, but often ran a few minutes late. If as I turned the corner of Wellington Street I heard the clank of the side rods of a slipping 'C13' class 4-4-2T as it struggled into my station, I might put on a spurt and board it so as to ride up to the terminus. Here a speedy reversal would be made and then back again as this was more comfortable than standing on a cold platform.

If the weather was very cold there would be no push-and-pull service due to 'technical problems'. On such occasions a 'J11' class 0-6-0 and two normal coaches would be pressed into use and we ran later than ever. One of the re-placement coaches certainly interested me as it was a third class non-vestibule, lavatory vehicle with the Hull & Barnsley coat of arms etched on the frosted lavatory window, not a common sort of coach.

I liked to catch the Stalybridge train at Guide Bridge if I could as this was often hauled by an 'A5' class 4-6-2 tank fresh off overhaul and the difference in acceleration over a 'C13' class was very noticeable. This would often use the slow lines as far as Fairfield but never once in my years of travel did I leave or board a train at the Gorton slow line platforms.

The following Hadfield train was my next means of conveyance a train which for quite a period was hauled by the unique 'N5' class 0-6-2T with extended side tanks, namely No. 5771, then stationed at Dinting Loco. My commuting journey was now more expensive as well as being earlier in the morning, as I no longer qualified for a staff free pass. I could, however, travel at privilege rate so I bought a pass covering journeys from Oldham to Manchester London Road which let me go to or from Ashburys on Openshaw Technical School days and was also valid on the LMS to or from Victoria or even Central, and this facility I retained throughout my days at Gorton.

Whilst in the machine shop I was often visited by Mr Ivors who would ask about my progress, and keep a fatherly eye on me, but one Monday I was saddened by the news that he had been on the line over the weekend and due to his deafness failed to hear an approaching train and so was knocked down and killed. His death was a great shock to the running department for he was universally liked and respected.

To turn now to a lighter affair altogether. In the vicinity of my centring machine were numerous automatic lathes of Herbert or Ward manufacture which were 'manned' by a bevy of young ladies who had been 'directed' to the Tank by the wartime labour regulations, and who worked not only overtime but also on a two shift system of a fortnight on days and then a similar period

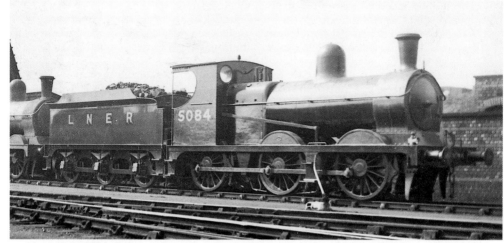

An early LNER footplate trip was on a 'J10' from Ince locomotive shed to Wigan Central and from there to Glazebrook. At this time in early 1943 around 10 such engines were allocated to the above shed. They were by no means in the first flush of youth as the first examples dated from 1892 being built by Kitsons, the last coming out of Gorton Tank in 1902 bringing the total up to 124.

A first driving lesson came on a 'J11' (GCR '9J') class 0-6-0. The 174 members of this class were true workhorses. Produced between 1901 and 1910 during which period 70 were built by Gorton Tank. Much later during my Gorton days about 21 were on our allocation and they never seemed to require over much attention despite intensive use on very varied work. One such duty was to haul the 7.16 am from Macclesfield to Manchester, noteworthy as being the only passenger train of the day not to call at Guide Bridge. Last stop was at Hyde Junction at 7.59 when a tender-first gallop to Manchester followed spoiled later by the insertion of an 8.07 am call at Gorton. I wonder just who was responsible for that? No. 64383 was a Gorton engine.

on nights. The hours reflected those of the day shift, i.e. start at 8.55 pm and finish if on overtime at 7.30 am which meant that the machines were in use for around 20 hours each day. Sometimes a girl would be off work for one reason or another when an apprentice would be put onto her lathe and one such temporary incumbent made an interesting discovery.

Beneath each lathe was a tray of cutting fluid, a sometimes milky, sometimes brown, oily liquid that travelled via a pump, pipe, tap and flexible hose to where it was wanted, namely the tip of the cutting tool. Usually if you failed to turn the tap off when you stopped the machine the system needed to be reprimed.

On this lathe it simply did not matter. Stop the motor, and keep the tap open over all lunchtime. Then return at the end of the hour, start up again and 'Hey presto' cutting fluid flowed and this unique facility set the young miscreant thinking.

Now although I have already mentioned the situation at starting time at the main time lodge, there was another ritual in each of the various shops. As 7.55 am or 1.30 pm came around a foreman would set out from his office and make a circuit of his domain. When you saw him in the distance, you put down your paper and either picked up your tools or started your machine. Machines had a switch box at their side. You put the main switch on, and then slowly pulled a vertically mounted handle over when the motor picked up speed, a violent yank at the handle not being appreciated. This young lady machine operator was usually only a few feet in front of the foreman at lunchtime, and then put the power on as quickly as possible, something that the temporary operator was banking on. He waited until she had disappeared at 12.30 towards the canteen, and then set the flexible pipe so that it pointed directly to the starting box, and disappeared in turn. As usual she raced down the shop, threw off her coat, and whipped the handle over when instantly a jet of oily coolant shot out from the nozzle and hit her drenching her overall. She promptly realised who the culprit was, saturated a handful of waste in the coolant trough, and foreman or no foreman set off in pursuit of the miscreant. It was quite an event, but eventually harmony was restored and work proceeded as usual. This in my experience was a very isolated incident as all the personnel seemed to get on well together, and certainly the senior turners would always come across and help the inexperienced with their problems.

I only had about three days on that centring machine and then I was put with an older apprentice who worked a Lang centre lathe to learn some of the intricacies of turning. He did quite a variety of work, and so was able to show me how to screw cut, or square centre, when as well as dealing with steel components we also taper-bored numerous cast-iron blast pipe tops.

I made several mistakes at first, for example put on 0.015 in. on the tool holder slide, and you reduce the diameter of the work, not by that amount, but by twice as much. But after two weeks or so I was reasonably proficient, and then given an adjacent almost identical Lang lathe but of smaller overall dimensions. It was then that I realised just how dangerous a tea break could be.

I was resetting the machine, so took off the four jaw chuck and replaced it with a faceplate and then inserted a driver in one of the slots on that component, when tea break followed. After the break I secured a driver to a mandrel, screwed my work to it, and started the lathe, having forgotten to tighten up the driver. As the machine gained some speed this flew off, whistled past my right ear, and hit the wall with sufficient force to put an indentation into the brickwork. Never again did I make such a mistake for had it hit me in the face I could well have been badly hurt.

I quite liked turning but then I was transferred to the tool room, to learn the art of milling and here again the same process occurred. I was initially put with the two shift operators of a large Parkinson machine, and then onto a smaller edition of the same make of miller. Here one had a regular reminder of what you should not do, for one of my two teachers had sometime earlier laid his hand on the table as it was traversing whilst he looked elsewhere when his hand and the cutter came into contact, and he lost a finger as a result.

The smaller miller was a nice machine though and whilst engaged on it I was shown how to set up and work a dividing head. The workmates were fine, but I did not like the tool room as it was partitioned off from the boiler shop by single tongue-and-groove boarding that did not reach the roof, so the noise within was far from pleasant. But no one in those now far off days thought of wearing ear protectors.

I was not sorry when yet another move took place, this time back into one of the high and much quieter bays, and onto yet another small Lang lathe. The task here was to produce motion rod pins for the 'rod job' located in the erecting shop at the top of four bay. It was manned by a chargehand, who appeared to do little work, and a leading hand who certainly did a lot. The latter a Mr McDowell was a psychologist who worked his art on me. He would arrive at my machine with a series of drawings usually pencilled on the back of cigarette packets, these showing all the requisite dimensions, the main body being to some micrometer size and all I had to do was to produce it from a piece of round steel bar of appropriate diameter. Pins were in demand, and one day I managed to give him 16 but then I had an idea and begged a high speed tipped tool off a relative who also worked in engineering but elsewhere. With that I could take faster and deeper cuts, and provide a much better finish on that all important dimension, and this gave me a little time to visit the rod job area of the erecting shop, and take an indirect route in the process to see what was happening in it.

I had some 10 months in total of lathe work, for part of this period 'setting up'. The girl operatives mentioned earlier worked on automatic lathes that turned out repetitive items such as studs or screws, etc. The machines and their tools had to be set to produce each separate batch of new components, and this provided a deal of experience as a variety of operations in a pre-determined sequence had to be followed and of course all the required component dimensions had to be met.

Machining eventually came to an end and I was transferred to the fitting benches to make a very significant discovery. You set up your machine and it did the work. But when fitting you set your job up, and then *you* did the work but here I was luckier than one of my friends whose fitting initiation came when he was presented with a radius gauge, a file, and a sizeable connecting rod, which had been machined with square corners along every one of its four long edges. He was then instructed to transform those 90 degree angles into neat, and to gauge radii. This was an exercise that did less than nothing for his morale, but an awful lot for his blisters.

At this time Gorton was overhauling the last 'B17' class 4-6-0s it was to see for some years, to the relief of the erecting shop staff who did not have a good word to say about them. This resulted in the works dealing in the main with either ex-GCR types or LNER-built 'J39s'. All of these had either Joy's gear in some older engines, or Stephenson's gear in the later ones, so eccentrics appeared in quantity from the erecting shop, being loosely put together therein. We pulled them apart and checked the condition of the studs on the front strap, the oil feed pipes in the oil wells, and the condition of the two long bolts which with their attendant nuts kept the assemblies *in situ* on their respective sheaves, these also being examined for faults.

The brass bearing housings were then remetalled in the white metal shop, and returned to us for reassembly before the white metal was machined to give the requisite run on the sheave. Then we had to clean up the end result, and provide washers on the bolts so that the top face of the securing nuts just lined up with the split pin holes which were provided with those items. An eccentric strap was then quite a heavy article and there was a knack in dropping them off the workbench, and then walking them to the area where the finished ones were kept ready marked up for return to the various erecting shop sections. As my immediate workmate, an eccentric in himself, dropped his completed specimen he would, for almost the first time for a lengthy period, actually speak saying with a deep sigh, 'Ah well it will come to no harm'. The other time when you could expect words was if he had some obstinate nut to deal with when he would say, 'Now come on, won't you come for Fred', only Fred was not his name. If the nut was stubborn he would then say 'Right then, take that' and apply some hefty hammer blows, when invariably the desired result occurred. We certainly had our characters!

I had 12 weeks on this type of work and then was moved to the cylinder section. Gorton had a very fine foundry which could and did produce the three in one 'monoblock' castings used on some North Eastern and GNR or LNER larger locomotives, but we did not see these as they were finished usually in the works that was their destination i.e. Darlington or Doncaster. The castings that came onto our section were for Great Central engines or for 'O4' 2-8-0 rebuilds that were just coming on stream, starting with No. 6595, or 3795 as it later became, these cylinders being of the 'B1' standard pattern.

All of these were marked out, machined, and so came to us to have all the sharp edges removed, any swarf extracted from the bores and ports, and then fitted with a multitude of studs all the associated holes having been drilled and tapped on the machines. Piston-valve cylinders also had to have liners fitted, and those to carry slide valves had to be checked for flatness of the working surface, and corrected where necessary. But thanks to more recent machines with their greater accuracy a lot of hand finishing that had been necessary in earlier years was no longer called for.

The next stage in a premium's education took place in the marking out section. There were three such tables positioned in the centre of one of the two

'Q4' class 0-8-0 No. 63201 light engine with the south wall of Gorton works as the backdrop. The two-storey part in the foreground is the end of a machine shop bay, the upper windows once lighting the former gallery. Then came the windows of the machine and boiler-mounting offices and the boiler steam test area. The wooden lean-to houses the drum, behind it is the drum's essential stationary boiler. Next came a part of the boiler shop and then the area where the copper stay lathes were located. The top floor of the end of the building housed the drawing office and on the far side the works manager's domain with the forge maintenance fitters workshop at ground floor level but quite out of sight. *W.A. Brown*

I well remember seeing a 'J11' class 0-6-0 being fitted on section 3 with new piston valve cylinders of the 'J39'-style. Here one such conversion, No. 64417, stands on Gorton Shed, now partially rebuilt. The brick wall in the background cut off short a stabling road to provide better working space in the new post-war fitting shop. Note the new paint on the lower part of the smokebox door. Burnt smokebox doors were often to be seen on Gorton's ex-GCR locomotives.

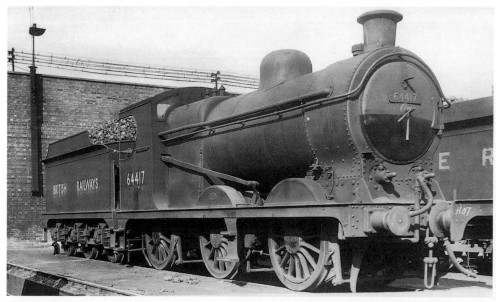

high bays by the entrance to the 'New fitting shop' where two more very competent hands, Charlie and Tommy, held sway.

With whitewash and a brush we coated the appropriate parts of some forging, casting or plate, and after setting it up square if such was required, used a scribing block to produce a centre line and from this scribed where the finished machined surfaces were to be, marking them with a centre punch, and similarly locating the points which would mark the centres of any holes to be put into the work.

Here accuracy was the order of the day when the ability to read a drawing properly was essential. It was a quiet occupation and once again our two seniors did all they could to show us how to deal with a whole variety of components.

By now my 15 months' stay in the machine and fitting shops was coming to an end and so I received orders to report to foreman Carter in the brass shop and thus found myself in the injector section, under leading hand Chamberlain.

Here face plate and under floor live steam injectors and the more complex exhaust steam injectors plus the associated water and steam supply valves were received from the erecting shop, stripped down, examined, had any worn or damaged parts replaced, and were then built up for further use. And here one had to wonder just how a series of cones and a mixture of cold water and steam could push that water at atmospheric pressure into a boiler working at 225 or 180 pounds per square inch. Injectors really were very ingenious devices. Now too for the first time one actually began to have jobs not on a component, but on a complete and possibly 'in steam' locomotive.

The latter situation could occur if some fault in the system was found when an engine was being tested after overhaul by our yard examiners or by the shed staff when it was initially returned to the Locomotive Running Department. Then with the defect note and a bag of tools in hand one left the shop to rectify the fault, which made a break from normal routine. I landed something rather different. Although we did not know it Austerity locomotives were coming in for checking over in readiness for the invasion and subsequent shipment to the continent. The work included sitting on top of a very cold boiler in an equally cold February, and grinding in the two clack valves located on top of that boiler in a brass casting. Now it would not have been a bad job had my subjects been brought into the shops but such sadly in most instances this was not the case, and after spending a morning so engaged a most positive numbness set in. After several weeks on injectors came a move to ejectors, the whole of Gorton's requirements being supplied by two long service hands. Or perhaps one and a half would be a more apt description as one gentleman was the OC of the works Home Guard company and so often disappeared to attend to some military duty. His colleague was very smart in appearance, very stern, and had no time for backsliding or incompetent apprentices. Under his relentless gaze you stripped an ejector down, spruced up nuts and other items on a brass lathe using hand tools in the process, ensured that the surfaces between the main casting and the banjo were making a well nigh perfect face to face joint, and completed a satisfactory rebuild in a minimum of time. But this was certainly the way to learn about ejectors and perhaps something else as well for my mentor acted as an old time dance MC, and so could with a little persuasion be coaxed into giving one a demonstration of the steps of the *Moonlight Saunter* or the *Pride of Eirean Waltz*. All fascinating stuff.

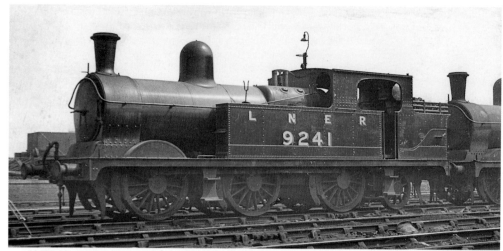

LNER No. 9241 was one of the 55 'N4' class 0-6-2 tanks built between 1889 and 1892. A Thomas Parker inspired design, all were fitted with Joy's valve gear. Six were built at Gorton the remainder by Neilson & Co. Very useful engines, No. 9241 had a long life, coming from Neilson's in May 1891 serving the MS&LR, the GCR, the LNER and ending its days in September 1949 as British Railways No. 69241. As can be seen its boiler is fitted with Ramsbottom safety valves so setting these was done in the yard with the locomotive in steam as described in the text.

At first sight No. 9369 could be just another 'N4', but not so as in 1891 Thomas Parker made two very significant changes to future 0-6-2 tank engine production fitting Stephenson's valve gear and a Belpaire firebox (on MS&LR No. 7) for the first time ever in Britain. In all 129 of these engines became LNER property in 1923, these being built up to 1901.

The next port of call for the premium apprentices was on the safety valve section, which again was staffed by just two skilled employees, who also had what could be described as 'an outside department'. Two sorts of valve were dealt with here, Ross 'pop', and Ramsbottom. It was initially the usual story, a labourer would come in pushing a barrow laden with valves removed from boilers, and our task was to strip them as necessary, check all the parts, and after grinding in the working faces, re-assemble them ready for setting, and here was a good part and a bad one. The former involved the Ramsbottom variety. With these you bolted the two vertical valve tubes to the boiler, and then popped the valves into the tubes. Next the spring anchor on the boiler was put in place and the nuts on the studs that held it screwed up part way. The spring and the bridge piece followed when those nuts were tightened sufficiently to hold the assembly in place, there being no spacing strip at this stage between the spring anchor and the boiler mounting face. When the boiler was being fired up for the yard engine test one of my two mates would be in attendance, having fixed a steam pressure test gauge *in situ*. Pressure would build up, and the anchor studs were then tightened down until the valves began to blow off at the desired pressure. Then a gauge cut into a series of steps was inserted between the spring anchor and the mounting face, and the thickness of the maximum possible insertion then recorded. When the boiler was cold again the spring anchor was removed once more, and a spacer equal to the clearance recorded between the anchor and the mounting put on the studs. The valve was then built up again and the studs wired and sealed to prevent unauthorised interference. This was a fairly noisy operation, but as pressure was generally fairly low and it all took place outside things could have been a lot worse. With Ross 'pops' they certainly were.

When a sufficient number of Ross valves had accumulated after rehabilitation they were barrowed by a labourer to that outside department or, to give it the name used in the shop, the 'drum'. This piece of equipment was situated in a wooden and glass lean-to against the main line side wall of the works.

The drum consisted of a circular steam receiver about six feet high and four feet in diameter. Around the upper edge was a wooden flooring, and in the centre a reducing valve, adaptor and a master pressure gauge. The drum was connected via a main steam pipe to a stationary boiler, and on 'Drum Days' this would be fired up and brought to full pressure, steam thus filling the receiver. You then lifted a valve onto the adaptor, and secured the several holding down bolts. Next open the reducing valve and the Ross 'pop' would start to blow off. With two long bent ring keys the safety valve setting and lock nuts were then manipulated until that safety valve was blowing off at the correct pressure, then it was removed and the next in the pile took its place.

Now Ross type valves blow off with quite a roar, and the setter was not only in a fairly small enclosure, but was also in very close proximity to them. Added to this as the afternoon progressed everything from drum to operator became hotter and hotter, and all this took place in an atmosphere redolent of a superior Turkish bath. The fact that one was easily able to see what was passing on the main line did little to ease one's discomfort and I for one was very glad when our various sessions on this apparatus came to their eventual end.

There was though one other similar 'treat' to be experienced. Every new or overhauled boiler was first given a cold water test, when with all the external

In the early summer of 1943 two sets of enginemen and a locomotive inspector would travel to Ordsall Lane once or twice a week to take over the first khaki-coloured Austerity 2-8-0 engines from the LMS men who had ferried them from the Vulcan Foundry where they were built. Gorton works then checked them over and they were run-in from the shed before being dispatched elsewhere. Vulcan built 390 of these engines between May 1943 and May 1945. A further 545 came from the Glasgow works of the North British Company. After the war some 200 were purchased as class 'O7' by the LNER. Grinding in those top clack valves, situated in the casting on the boiler top midway between the chimney and the dome, in the winter of 1944 was a very cool experience. This view shows No. 78634 at Doncaster in June 1946. *T.G. Hepburn/Rail Archive Stephenson*

After the Vulcan-built Austerities came the US Army Transportation Corps 'S.160' class 2-8-0 engines which were very different from anything else to be seen at Gorton. After their voyage across the Atlantic quite a lot of attention was necessary including putting on the valve gear, before they could be dispersed elsewhere. I do not now know just how many passed through the Tank, but nearly 400 came to be sent to the UK before being dispatched to the Continent after the June 1944 invasion. I was often on them but never had a footplate trip as none were retained at Gorton Shed. No. 2415 is seen passing Hatch End in 1944 with a down freight. *C.R.L. Coles/Rail Archive Stephenson*

connections blanked off it would be pressured up to some fixed figure over the normal working pressure, a process that would find any weak spots, when leaks were marked with yellow wax chalk for subsequent rectification. Then came a live steam test.

The boiler would be seated on a stillage, and filled with water to the usual working level. Then a fire would be put in the grate and pressure built up. Again an overload test was carried out, when one shinned up a ladder, laid down an asbestos mat and sitting on this tightened down the safety valves until the test pressure was reached.

This was, to say the least, interesting, and time could not be wasted as having no injector connections no further water could be put into the boiler once action was in progress. After this, and by way of a complete change, came the only job in the works where one was allowed to sit down to attend to the tasks in hand, stools even being provided.

This was on the gauge bench, where again just two skilled workmates examined, repaired and tested every pressure and vacuum gauge used by Gorton works. The theory behind pressure gauges was very simple. A tube bent into an arc was at one end connected to the working medium, whilst at the other and sealed end was a link to a gear which in turn was connected to the pointer. As pressure rose the bent tube formed to a radius tried to straighten itself, the movement then being transmitted via the link and gear to the pointer so registering the pressure on the dial.

Brass shop work was in the main reasonably light, reasonably clean, and apart from the 'drum' interesting and acceptable. But once again after nine months I was told to move on yet again and so my wallet number that had changed to 2866 when I went into the brass shop changed once more to 3053 for now I was to become acquainted with the art of boiler mounting.

Yet again I had to introduce myself to a new foreman, in this case Mr Rathbone, and remember my new wallet number as I passed through the time lodge. Boiler mounting took place in more than one location, and so I was directed initially to bay four in the erecting shop where the chargehand told me to work with Bob Stephenson, who proved to be a super mate. The boilers that we had to deal with had been stripped of their tubes, but still retained the front tubeplate, the foundation ring and the copper firebox, with all its scores of stays. Plating, tubing and riveting were the province of the boilermaking staff, but nuts, bolts, washers, etc., indicated tasks for the fitters. Outside each boiler we made sure that the handrail mountings were secure, and ready for the erectors to fit the stanchions, ensured the faces for the various valves and other fittings were in proper order, and die-nutted all the studs that were to be re-used, or replaced any that seemed to be in any way dubious - worn threads, or loose in their sockets. Then we added all the brasswork, faceplate injectors, steam supply valves, the combination stand superheater header and the exterior regulator fittings, but there was also internal work to be accomplished, and so one had to learn the art of insinuating oneself into the boiler.

You did this by climbing via a wooden ladder to the top, and then lowering a six inch plank, slightly less in length than the diameter of the boiler, on a piece of rope down the open dome, and then manipulating it so that it came to rest below the dome and across the boiler. Then you lowered yourself downwards, so that your feet came to rest on the plank, then you could duck and step into the interior. Some illumination could well be necessary, but nowhere in Gorton at that time were there any low voltage handlamps, a paraffin flare would have been too smoky, so it was either a gas jet, or a candle, but the former gave off heat, the latter little light, so the choice was not an easy one to make. Inside the boiler were the main steam pipe running from dome to front tube plate and just below the dome the mounting for the regulator valve. The valves were overhauled in the machine/fitting shop by a fitter or two who seemed to do nothing else, but placing the valve *in situ*, and inserting the regulator rod, and making sure the whole assembly worked was done by the boiler mounters. They also had to ensure that any other internal pipes were secure and in order for the work they had to do. When the internal jobs had been finished or it was break or lunch time, self extraction was necessary, and getting through the taller but smaller diameter domes of the older engines could be an interesting exercise. If you wanted to be a successful boiler mounter, it paid to have a lean and lithe figure. I should add here that the boilers at this stage were tubeless , the carcass passing after the boiler mounters had finished to boilermakers for tubing.

I enjoyed my time with Bob for he was one of the nicest men that I came to work with, whilst working conditions in four bay were also very acceptable. But then I was moved onto the boiler marking-out section which was in the main boiler shop opposite the partitions of the tool room and was even noisier than it was in that place.

Gorton, as well as making boilers for ex-GCR locomotives, was now engaged on the production of '100A', or 'B1' type boilers for 'O1' rebuilds, for 'O4/8' conversions, and for supply to other LNER workshops, e.g. Darlington and Doncaster. The boiler and firebox shell all complete was brought over by overhead crane, and lowered into a fixture made up from substantial steel members. Then it was levelled up so that the centre of the boiler and the top faces of the fixture were truly parallel, when marking out could commence. This work had of necessity to be very accurate, but what also was accurate was the way in which the platers and boilermakers could roll and punch substantial steel plates, so that any variation from the dimensions shown on the drawings was of the absolute minimum. I had several weeks on this job, and then came yet another move to the mounting bay, directly behind the wall fronting the main line, a wall which also supported the lean-to housing the drum.

Then came yet another and long distance move to the newer section of works to have a spell in the millwright's department. Foreman George Wright had a chat with me, and then his No. 2 Mr Rankin led me to the steam crane section and left me in the care of chargehand Pearson. The steam crane repair gang were a cheery lot, and well they needed to be for by the time any crane came in for overhaul and their attentions it could safely be classed as being well worn.

The cranes I saw made by such firms as Smiths or Booths of Rodley near Leeds were quite complex, as they could not only lift or slew, but were also self-propelling, and so had a boiler, an engine, several sets of gears, winding drum and ropes, and, of course, the essential controls.

The boilers were taken away for repair in the appropriate parts of the works, but the rest of the assembly was left to the crane gang, and one task I remember was to look over every gear wheel, and see if there were any worn or broken teeth. If any such faults extended to only a minimal number, then the offending 'tushy pegs' were chiselled off to the root, and a series of drilled and tapped holes placed along the centre line. Studs were then screwed in, and thereafter built up with welding, when one took up a file and profile gauge and brought the end result back as near as possible to the original profile. All this would doubtlessly horrify any gear cutting professional, but as I have said these cranes were pretty well worn, and such repairs seemed to do the job surprisingly well. In some respects crane work gave one an inkling as to what life in the erecting shop might be like, but that was still to come. There was another branch of the crane repair facility that dealt with all the overhead cranes but it was obviously felt that premium apprentices should keep their feet firmly on the ground so we were never allocated to that gang.

The millwright's shop was as I have said in the 'new works' which also housed other departments. There were a boiler shop, an area used by the permanent way people to lay out new point and crossing assemblies, the spring shop and the tender shop.

Amongst the select band of workers who left the plant every night at 5.15 pm was a springsmith, Arthur by name, who must have been well over retirement age, and so kept on by virtue of the wartime emergency. I went in to see him a few times for he was a friendly soul; as we passed each night through the time lodge he would sigh and say, 'That's once more, once less'. But despite his age he could manhandle the very heavy locomotive springs, and it was interesting to watch him at work, although the smell that came off some of the oil quenching vats was not something that I could appreciate. The tender shop too was not a place that normally saw a premium apprentice within its confines. Of the eight or so of us who were then going the rounds of the works, only one was given the privilege, we thought it a dubious one, of having a spell in there, when sadly we tended to pull his leg about the move.

After steam cranes I had a short spell with two or three fitters, who did almost any general work that came along, and then was moved back to the original part of the works to join the forge gang, who occupied a workshop adjacent to the works manager's office. The remit here was to maintain the drop stamps, the mechanical forging machines and the steam hammers that ranged from a very large hammer to a series of smaller ones. Many of the latter were to be found in the nearby roundhouse that had been the original Gorton locomotive shed, and then had a unique two-road turntable turning around the large centre roof column. All trace of this had long since been removed, and now around the circular walls were smiths hearths, and anvils, each with an adjacent steam hammer now operated by some member of the female sex who certainly seemed to know how to control their charges. Also on the maintenance list were the oil fired furnaces, used either for heating components, or for annealing them. One of our tasks was to patrol their locations at starting up time to ensure that all was well, when the atmosphere was to say the least decidedly thick.

The forge department was at this time very busy doing work not only for Gorton, but for other concerns such as nearby Crossley Motors. For the first time I found myself working all day on Saturdays and Sundays, when getting to Gorton by bus was something of a trial, there being no Sunday trains from

Wheel shop equipment was substantial. Here a crank axle is being reconditioned, whilst in the background a wheel set is undergoing tyre turning. A crank shaft was a sizeable component. No wonder I found commercial vehicle repair work far easier on one's muscles.

Oldham to Guide Bridge. The works too seemed strangely quiet, but to most of the staff working on these days was the accepted norm when circumstances so demanded. For example in my time the largest steam hammer suffered a major failure and quite a complex repair had to be undertaken. After some weeks with chargehand Bob Hart and his men I was told to move once more to join the very select band who maintained all the works' high pressure hydraulic system, and who had a very cosy 'hidyhole' against the circular wall of the roundhouse.

The hearts of the hydraulic system were the two sets of pumping engines one located near to our cosy billet, the other and much grander set being in a house over at the new works. These units pumped water into their accumulators, which consisted of a boiler like structure mounted vertically in a framing, and attached to a substantial piston which had several feet of vertical movement. The boiler was heavily weighted, the pumps forcing water under the piston, which together with the 'boiler' was then forced upwards to the end of the determined travel when the pump power was automatically cut off. As the shops used hydraulic power the accumulator assembly fell to the point where the pumps tripped in again and the cycle was repeated.

I gathered that an attempt had been made earlier to connect the two systems by laying a main across the works yard but this had been none too successful, and certainly in my time each worked independently. We did some pipe work, though, as now and again a piece or a joint would fail, sometimes with spectacular results, when a dig ensued to reach the offending location. The pressure in the system was very high but sadly now I cannot remember just what were the pounds per square inch recorded on the gauges.

Hydraulic power was used in many sections of the works, so we made excursions all over the premises to renew piston seals, or attend to other tasks and nowhere did one find a more spectacular hydraulic result than in the wheel shop. Here wheels were pressed on or off axles, and the force needed to effect removal by the ram on the axle end could often exceed 20 tons, when a penetrating 'crack' announced that separation had begun. The wheel shop was another interesting place with its huge wheel lathes turning remorselessly as a cutting tool brought a new tyre to the right profile. Here was work of a very demanding nature, and the men who had charge of these sizeable machines really knew their craft. Certainly being in charge of one for the first time must have been quite daunting.

I was in the wheel shop one morning when, after finishing my job, decided to pop into the erecting shop to have a word with one of my confrères who had been moved into it a few days before, he having had that tender shop experience mentioned earlier. By this time I had frequently walked through the place, looking at what locomotives were coming in or going out, but had not taken over much notice of the workforce, but this morning was different.

I found my friend's one bay section and then located him under an engine with heavily soiled overalls, and a face and hands that were in just the same condition. He looked at me in an appealing manner, when I asked just how he had got into that condition he simply replied, 'It's the job'. It made me wonder about what the future in that part of the works would bring knowing full well that in due course I would be finding out, when my 4669 millwright's wallet number would change yet again.

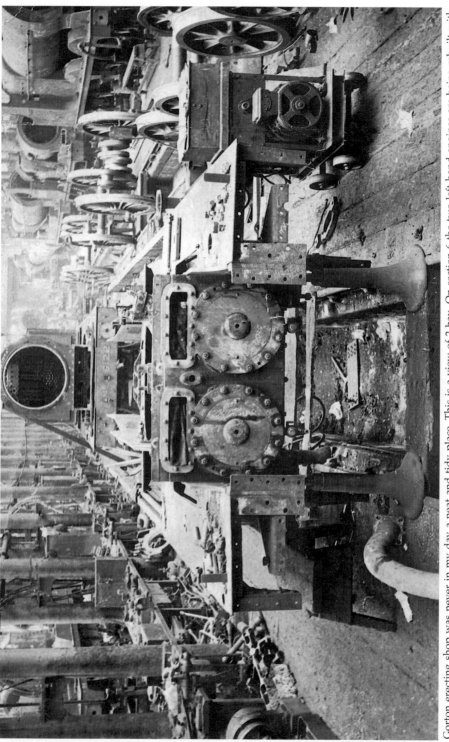

Gorton erecting shop was never in my day a neat and tidy place. This is a view of 2 bay. On section 6 the two left-hand engines are being rebuilt with perhaps a 'C13' in the foreground and 'C14' No. 6122 behind. Being stripped on the right-hand side are a 'J11', a 'J10', an 'O4' and an 'N5'. The trolley in the foreground carries the sort of electric welding set that was around in my day. The centre road is where wheels were removed and replaced and where axlebox fitting took place.

Chapter Seven

Locomotives Unlimited

Needless to say my turn duly came, and so on the 14th December I reported to Mr Hatton the chief foreman whose jurisdiction extended to both the machine and erecting shops, so that I could gain my experience in the latter. Before I go into details let me first describe this most important part of the works.

The shop had five bays, number one bay having windows along its length these forming a part of the exterior wall that lay parallel to the main line. At the inner end of the bay was a raised platform on which were positioned the foremen's offices, and the drawing stores. A flight of wooden steps led down from the platform to the main shop floor and so into the realm of section one, where in earlier years new locomotives had been constructed. Passing down the bay and beyond this first section one came to a wide crossing equipped with a set of rails that ran at right angles across the whole width of the erecting shop. Beyond the crossing as one approached the outer doors came sections two, three and four.

Two bay was basically similar, at the top was section five, then came the crossing and then sections six, seven, and eight. Bay three began with section nine, then came the crossing once more, and after it sections, 10, 11 and 12.

Four bay was laid out rather differently. At the top instead of locomotives came the area occupied by the rod job. Next was a partitioned-off stores area where one could obtain such items as nuts, bolts and washers, or split pins, and on the outer side of the crossing was the boiler mounting area where I had worked previously, this taking up the space that would otherwise have accommodated two locomotive sections. This left sufficient space to house section 13 hard by the main doors, only the men here spent most of their days undertaking light repairs and rectifying accident damage so most of their subjects came and went with some rapidity.

Five bay was different again, as it only ran from the crossing down to the main doors, and this was full not of locomotives but boiler holding cradles. The whole bay was given over in my time to the boilermakers, who were overhauling these essential components, and making more than a little din in the process, but as the erecting shop was quite lofty one did not suffer from the noise aspect as was the case when, say, in the toolroom. This shortening of bay five provided, on the other side of the dividing wall, an extension to the wheel shop.

The main crossing now continued across the top of the wheel shop and gave access via a sloping ramp to the works yard, passing as it did the copper shops and the steamy 'bosche' where greasy parts taken off locomotives were cleaned before being passed to the machine and fitting departments. You will gather from what is set down here that the erecting shop floor was at a lower level than the floor of the machine shop, and so almost in line with the bay four rod job was another wooden ramp that allowed the works Lister trucks to run from one level to the other. At the top were to be found the tanks holding that 'mystic' cutting fluid I have mentioned earlier. From the foot of this ramp, and equal to it in width, was a space running across to the aforementioned foreman's office platform, a space that had originally housed the steam engines that powered the rope drives of the overhead cranes. But engines and ropes had now vanished as all the cranes had electric drive that must have eased their maintenance very considerably. Each bay had a wooden baulk floor and three lines of rails, every line being provided with a pit having brick sides and a concrete floor. As you looked down the shop from the main doors the central set of tracks received incoming engines which were there de-wheeled. The rest of the assembly was then swung onto the left-hand set of pits to stand on four substantial screw jacks in readiness for stripping. In theory at least all the dirt was kept to one side of the bay. When this process was completed the frame assemblies were swung over to the right-hand tracks where rebuilding took place, and when the appropriate stage was reached it was back into the centre once more for re-wheeling and final completion.

Each bay had a bay foreman who seemed to be more of a parts chaser than a staff controller, and each section was made up of a chargehand, about 12 fitters, two apprentices and two labourers. Let it be said that for most of the employees their section formed their world as one had little discourse normally with men on other sections even the one next door to you. A section normally had four locomotives on its patch at any one time, two of these being on the stripping side, the other two building, and as soon as one went out another quickly took its place.

Engines were not the only thing to head towards those large shop doors that gave access to the erecting shop yard. One day a gang of platelayers arrived and began to lift a part of that wooden floor, then in were shunted several bogie flat wagons. From a sizeable cavity below the floor the overhead cranes produced a number of large naval gun barrels that must have been in store for some years. Now Gorton had a dry dock. This formed a part of the barge repair section that was located against the sponge cloth laundry and connected with the Stockport branch of the Ashton canal, but I never saw any of the boats receiving attention therein fitted with a piece of 16 in. naval ordnance.

To return though to the erecting shop. It and the rest of the works were not exactly laid out on 'flow line principles'. For example if a boiler coming off an engine located in section 11 was to be repaired in the main boiler shop then one of the two cranes in bay three would pick it up and take it to the crossing. There it would be swung through 90° and put on a trolley running on the crossings track. The trolley was then pushed as far as one bay where another crane picked it up once more, swung it again through another right-angle and carried it to the foreman's office platform where another trolley on another set of rails would be waiting. These rails ran through both bays of the machine shop, and now came the clever bit. A boiler shop crane would come as close to the machine shop as it could and a long rope would be run from it to the trolley. Off would head the crane in the Gorton station direction, and as the slingers made sure no one was in the way the trolley and its load trundled likewise under horizontal rather than vertical crane power. All very quaint but quite effective, and time and labour consuming. Some ex-erecting shop boilers were destined for the shop in the 'new' part of the works so they had to be taken to the erecting shop yard after being loaded on a truck, and then shunted to their destination.

My erecting shop spell began when Mr Hatton passed me on to foreman Tommy Williams who along with his partner Mr Whittaker oversaw the whole shop. He promptly dived into a cupboard and fished out a selection of tools which were to say the least vintage as most were stamped 'MS&L', so they were then at least 40 years old and one of these fortunately attracted the attention of a stranger who was in the office at the time. Fortunately, because I had no idea as to its purpose. This tool had a chisel-like body that was drawn to a point at the business end, only about 1½ in. before that point was reached the body was bent through some 45° to the main axis. Tommy demonstrated how it was used to extract split pins and then told me to put this remarkable collection of railway antiques into a sack and find the section four chargehand, by name of Harry Norris, and tell him that I had been allocated thereto for some time to come.

Section four was of course to be found in one bay against those main doors, this bay being unlike the others in that it boasted not two overhead cranes but three, and strengthened crane runs as well. This extra provision was due to an earlier intention to have all the heavier locomotives repaired on sections one to four inclusive. This no longer seemed to apply, where a repair job went depended on what space became available. I quickly found myself on the stripping side where compound Atlantic *Viscount Cross* was in the process of being reduced to a set of parts. The fitter I was put with suggested that I could make a start by removing the splashers which were sizeable assemblies as they had to accommodate the engine's 6 ft 9 in. diameter driving wheels.

The splashers were kept in place by numerous bolts of around ⅝ in. diameter that passed through both flanges riveted to the side of the splashers, and the footplate framing. Everyone had a nut and a lock nut plus a split pin, and every one was rusted in the extreme being most definitely loose. The only way to deal with them was to trap the bolt head by inserting a chisel between the head and the splasher side, and hoping it would stay put whilst one tried to unscrew the nuts, after of course cutting off the head and tails of the split pin. *Viscount Cross* was standing on the usual four screw-type holding jacks so my head was of necessity up inside the splasher where light was conspicuous by its absence. I struggled but my next stripping task was a lot worse. When an engine came in it was lifted by the cranes until the axleboxes came to rest on the horn stays, thus taking the weight off the springs. The spring pins could now be knocked out, the engine lowered, and with the horn stays and brake rods, etc., no longer *in situ* another lift left the wheel assemblies behind and the subject ready to be swung to the stripping area and those four holding stands.

Each spring pin passed through the upper end of an adjustable spring bolt but these remained within their respective spring hanger brackets and so needed to be removed. Here again were nuts, lock nuts and split pins plus a vibration damper. This was an open-ended cast-iron box filled with a thick rubber pad which fitted between the spring hanger bracket and the adjusting nut, but the rubber did not quite fill the box, leaving room for a flat filler plate that also was equipped with a securing device. The easy way would have been

When I first met *Viscount Cross* on section four of the Gorton erecting shop 'he' was not in such an immaculate condition. Removing the four driving wheel splashers proved to be an interesting experience but in due course, put together again, it was hauled into the yard there to undergo its steam test and receive a coat of our gas tar paint substitute, when lining was conspicuous by its absence, as was polished brasswork.

The 'S1' 0-8-4 tank engines were big and so were their side tanks. Their filling holes were top front, the balance pipes to the bunker tank with their fixing bolts bottom back. Between the two were a series of baffles some fixed to the tank top, some to the tank bottom. Now reader imagine yourself, candle in one hand and tools in the other, making your way across for a spot of bolt fixing. As you do, ask yourself the question: When was the tank last cleaned? Ever?

to have simply burned off the bolts but this was not permitted so it was simply a case of undoing ('Ha-Ha') the nuts that possessed yet another well rusted thread only this was of around 2¼ in. diameter Whitworth thread and each bolt was loose in those hanger brackets.

A bar long enough to go from one side of the frame assembly to the other was inserted through the pin hole in the bolthead one elected to work on first plus its opposite number, thus preventing either from turning. Then you laced the threads with as much penetrating oil as possible, took up a heavy single-ended spanner, added a pipe to the plain end to provide additional torque, and sweated. If success was not forthcoming play a gas jet on the nut, hoping that, when sufficiently hot, expansion would ease matters only now the rubber in the box would begin to melt and so your efforts took place in a very heady atmosphere.

By the end of my first day I realised that to be a success on the stripping side you needed to be a pocket Hercules, and alas I was not in that class. I spent a few weeks on the stripping side but my nadir came one Monday morning when 'B7' class 4-6-0 No. 1361 came in. Harry kindly decided that I might try my hand at stripping out the smokebox, and here was a treat in store. To begin the smokebox which had not been emptied had to be put through that process, so one of the labourers and I spent a deal of the morning removing a large quantity of soot and ash before the real business could begin. Now a 'B7' or 'Black Pig' had four cylinders, so the smokebox was nicely filled with steam bends (main steam pipes from the header to the valve chests), a blastpipe with two additional side legs, an ash ejector (when was that last used?), blastpipe top and blower connections, and last but not least a superheater header and its attendant elements. As I surveyed this collection Harry came up to tell me that stripping *did not* mean scrapping and so if I were to break any of the cast-iron parts my popularity would be less than 'zilch'. I made a start only to find that whereas it was normal to build up boxes using brass nuts this one was equipped throughout with the steel variety so in every case it was necessary to use a hammer and chisel to split them as they were so corroded. Each time I struck a blow of course a cloud of soot descended from the upper regions and in no time at all I was well and truly blackened from head to foot.

The job took me almost a whole week as someone at a shed had stopped a bottom blastpipe joint blow by covering the area with a layer of cement, most of which had to be laboriously chipped away before one could even see the holding down nuts. I was thoroughly fed up by Saturday, but then Harry firmly indicated that this sort of progress was not good enough for him and consequently when No. 1381 came in for a Monday morning start I could start stripping out yet another smokebox, on yet another 'B7' four-cylinder.

In almost 60 years at work No. 1361 gave me my worst ever week, and when in later years the staff were out on strike, or passenger recession was beyond estimate, or the council members were not being helpful, I would look at the photograph of the beast that I kept by me for the purpose and come to the immediate conclusion that life really wasn't bad after all!

As it transpired No. 1381 did have brass nuts and *no* cement so I finished the task by Wednesday morning when Harry indicated he was satisfied and I became involved in removing the clothing plates. To do this you eased off the

My *bête noir*. Here is the photograph I kept by me for years to remind me how work could be a real heartbreaker. Stripping out the smokebox was a task that I never forgot. No. 1361 was built at Gorton being the second '9Q' class to take the rails in June 1921 as GCR No. 73, later becoming No. 5073 as a 'B7' in LNER stock.

encircling straps, climbed on top, and removed carefully all the securing set screws, easing up the top edge of each plate in turn, fixing a G-clamp *in situ*, adding a rope sling, and then having an overhead crane come along and swing the plate clear after all the hand rails had been removed. Their support columns fitted into mountings secured to the side of the boiler, but these could not be unbolted as they were beneath the plating so one had to punch out the taper pins that kept the assemblies together, but often the lower edge of a pin would lie beneath the plates, and so gaining access to them in order to knock them upwards was more than a mite difficult.

Once the plating was away the 'crinolines' could be removed together with the asbestos mats that surrounded the boiler and in so doing prevented some loss of heat. Each piece was marked up in chalk as it was freed so that those who would later find themselves putting it all together again would have some idea as to which bit went where. As you yourself might well come to fall for that job it was as well to take as much care as possible in ensuring prompt identification. After these sorts of exercises taking down motion or removing pistons was almost a doddle.

Harry now decided that I had better move over onto the building side so he put me with Joe Bromley, one of the senior fitters, who was another excellent mate and tutor. Joe was, however, a leading light in the union and so would often leave to attend some urgent meeting or other after first indicating the work he wanted me to do whilst he was away. Invariably thanks to Joe's frequent absences most of the jobs we did took place around the rear end of our subjects putting in place the many pipes that supplied steam to various valves and injectors plus sand gear, lubricator pipes, and the lubricators themselves. Here one needed experience and that Joe had in full measure.

As the piping was removed on the stripping side, it was piled into a heap that was then removed by the labourers to the copper shop for repair and subsequent annealing. It was then returned to the building side, the basic frame assembly having by this time moved over, and so once again a pile of mixed, very mixed, copper piping was to be found usually somewhere in the middle of the section patch. The question now was, which piece goes where? Joe, however, never had a problem here as he could virtually recognise every piece at a glance and could do the necessary when we received in error a pipe that had not been removed originally from one of our subjects. Here, though, was another problem for the young enthusiast. We all knew what a 'C13', or a 'B4', or a 'J10' looked like but in the erecting shop, and indeed most of the works, the Grouping had never occurred so what I knew as a 'B7' was no such thing, it was a '9Q' whilst an 'O4' was an '8K' and don't you forget it! Still as 'J39s' and 'B17s' were post-1923 productions they were at least always so identified.

I decided that I had had my fill of 'back ends' so I suggested to Joe that a change onto the front would be welcomed. He agreed and we started to put together the pistons, valves, and valve gear of a 'J39', and at length reached the stage where the valves needed setting. Joe took me through this part of the proceedings, but came to the conclusion that one of the eccentric rods was rather too long and thus needed shortening. Here I had another lesson in basic engineering, for he told me to take it to the smithy and have it reduced by a ¼ inch. Well Joe was not the sort of man to play a trick on an innocent apprentice so I shouldered the rod and made my way to that old Sheffield, Ashton-under-Lyme & Manchester roundhouse where the smiths were located.

Now as all this took place over 50 years ago my remembrance of actual dimensions is a bit hazy but as I recall it this rod was about 4 ft long. At one end was the foot shaped like a 'T' with two holes bored in it to accommodate the eccentric sheaves holding studs. The main body was around 1¼ in. thick and about 4 inches deep whilst at the other end the metal was forged into a pair of jaws which were also bored to accept a motion pin. Now in my view the way to shorten that rod was to machine the requisite amount off the foot but there I was very wrong.

On arrival at the smithy I outlined my desire to the foreman who directed me to one of the smiths standing by his hammer, each hammer having a team consisting of the smith himself, a girl hammer driver and a male striker but on this occasion the latter two were superfluous to the task in hand. The smith laid the rod on his anvil, picked up a steel rule and a scriber and drew a line in the middle of the main body. Then with a centre punch he made two 'pop' marks about 10 inches apart on that line. He then set a pair of dividers to the marks, turned up the air supply to the fire in his hearth, and when the coke was glowing with heat put the part of the rod where his line was into the hottest part of his fire. Soon the rod was cherry red, and after putting on a pair of leather gloves he took the rod out of the fire and gave the 'T' end two or three very solid thumps on the smithy floor. But before this took place he said to me 'Quarter of an inch son, bare or full?' I hadn't a clue but replied, 'Full', thinking that if need be a piece of packing could always be inserted between the foot and the eccentric sheave. We waited till the rod had cooled then he checked with his dividers how the distance between his two marks had been reduced, and also that the hole in the jaw end was square with those in the foot.

There was after this exhibition no doubt in my mind that Gorton had some highly skilled craftsman and as my experienced broadened so did my respect for them increase. Then came my 'black week'.

Joe was off somewhere that Monday morning so I was told to work with a new fitter who was starting with us for the very first time after having been demobilised from the services. Our job was to cut off some seized bolts using a seven pound hammer and set chisel and I took up the hammer. This - though - did not suit my new mate who, after inquiring how old I was, said in no uncertain terms that *he* was the journey man and so holding the wire handle of the chisel would be my task whilst he wielded the hammer. He took a mighty swipe, completely missing the chisel head, when seven pounds of metal hit the side of the frame, bounced back, and made immediate contact with my head. I saw stars, and hit the floor but we were tough in those days so as a large bump swelled up I made my way right across the works to that most recent innovation, our well equipped ambulance room. It was a basic necessity in my view in that works. The nurse on duty was most unsympathetic, as she cut away a chunk of hair and applied a plaster. I returned to section four to carry on with the day's work.

Then came Tuesday. Deciding that working solo did have advantages, I moved back to the back end of our '8K' or 'O4' in more modern parlance, and started removing the pipework as this engine was on the stripping side. Like all other Gorton natives it had a wooden cab floor and the task of either taking these up, or subsequently replacing them fell to the joiners. One member of this fraternity was engaged in lifting the floor, but alas there was a fire brick firmly wedged between the back of the firebox and the boiler end of the floor. As he prised the boarding up, he freed the brick which would have reached the floor of the pit thanks to gravity if only my head had not been in the way. Well he did call out 'below' but only after the brick had started its downwards descent, so I had another trip to our first aid department. There the nurse after gently inquiring if I made a habit of this sort of thing, cut off some more hair, and added a matching plaster, as the brick with kindly forethought did manage to hit the then undamaged side of my forehead.

By some miracle I left the works on Wednesday evening after a full and incident free session in the erecting shop, caught as usual the 5.27 pm from Gorton station and there changed onto the 5.42 pm to Oldham Glodwick Road that was already standing at its platform. As usual the push-and-pull set had the inevitable two coaches, and the one I made for was a downgraded ex-first class compartment vehicle that did offer very comfortable travel. The open saloon with its driver's compartment was a coach I never patronised but this night that was certainly a pity.

Two elderly ladies were already occupying the platform side window seats as I boarded so I moved to take up a facing seat across from them and so settled down for the 16 minute ride to Oldham Clegg Street my destination, but my normally peaceful contemplation of the route came to be disturbed somewhat after only five minutes after the train pulled out from Guide Bridge.

My fellow passengers wished to alight at Ashton Oldham Road the first stop, but could not manage to open the door so they appealed to me for help. This coach had slide locks, but it was wooden-bodied, and that door was certainly a tight fit and was not going to open easily. Under such circumstance the easy way was to drop the door window and turn the outside handle, only snag there was no window strap. By now my travelling companions were becoming agitated not wanting to be taken on to Park Bridge, so I took a firm hold on the slide pushed it as far over as possible, and after putting my shoulder to the door gave it a hard 'bump'. The results were entirely unexpected.

The Oldham train was not over worked. On weekdays at this period there was no service from Guide Bridge to Oldham from 8.50 am to 3.30 pm although two intermediate trips were provided on Saturdays, Sunday being entirely devoid of trains as the service on that day had been suspended at the outbreak of the war.

Consequently the stock spent a lot of time standing in the siding at Guide Bridge as had been the case this wet afternoon when previously some passenger had left that window down. Net result as I pushed my feet slipped on a saturated floor, I lost my balance , and with a resounding crash shattered the window. At Clegg Street the damage was duly noted, and my name was taken for the foreman there knew I worked at Gorton. Some days later I had to see Mr

Simpson in his office and explain why I had come to damage a part of the company's property. Fortunately he readily accepted my explanation, asked about my still bruised forehead, and in somewhat humourous tones agreed it had not been a very successful week. Nor had it really been a very profitable one for according to my diary my wage for the relevant period had come to all of £2 0s. 2d.

As I have said previously the first aid room was a new and much appreciated innovation, because the general nature of the work in the 'Tank' meant that the staff were bound to suffer from various minor injuries. But the events of the morning of 15th March, 1946, were way beyond its abilities. That Friday morning Joe and I were working on a set of almost bare frames positioned on the stripping side of our section. There was another of our subjects partially stripped behind us, whilst in front actually on section three was a large tank locomotive also somewhat dismembered. We were sitting on a plank cleaning up the rear inside cylinder faces of our subject whose number has now escaped my memory, whilst over to our left the boilermakers in five bay were riveting away with gusto and making copious noise in the process. All at once there was a muffled 'thump' followed a second or so later by one or possibly two more, our frames rocked on their four jacks and a dense cloud of smoke began to envelope us.

We came out from under those frames at high speed and began to make our way through the murk towards the shop crossing when suddenly Joe turned, stopped me and said, 'Get back Geoff and for God's sake don't look'. I did as I was bid and we arrived in the open air via the main shop doors. Unknown to us a member of the boiler shop staff had been using an oxyacetylene gas set to burn off some bolts on the tank engine in front of us, the gas bottles being, as was usual at that time, laid on a four-wheeled cart in the horizontal position.

Unfortunately the regulator assembly must have developed a fault, as a fire began to develop in that area. The foreman over the relevant staff saw what was occurring and rushed to help, but then the end came off the bottle and the ensuing blast killed both men. The bottle then rocketed down the aisle to reach the crossing where it exploded, where at least two more men were killed and where our own chargehand Harry was so badly injured as to lose both his legs.

I never knew just what it was that Joe had seen, I never asked him and he never told me, but what was certain was that the shop staff were shaken to the core and work promptly and rightly ended for the day. Some few days later many of us lined the pavements of Cornwall Street as a funeral cortège of one of the victims passed. At this point one can only wonder as to what would have subsequently happened if the present Health & Safety Legislation had then been in force. After this most tragic affair bottles were always mounted vertically and I for one treated them with the greatest of respect for the rest of my career.

One former erecting shop task we were spared in my time was that of having to walk heavy axle boxes up a plank, putting them onto their journals to mark them for fit, and then scraping up the white metalled brass, until a suitable working surface was achieved. Now much more accurate boring machines did the job for you, but one still had to lift each box into its hornway, put the hornstay in place, and then set up the wedges with which many ex-GC engines were fitted before wheeling could take place. Another regular task was to remove any defective studs from the cylinder castings, when those that lay in the smokebox would frequently be in a poor condition. We did have stud extractors, but often the stud would fail to come out or shear off. Then the residue or complete stud was cut off flush with the cylinder face, a pop mark was put into the centre, and a hole was then drilled down the stud remains whose diameter was slightly under the root diameter of the attendant thread. Then with a round nose chisel, the residue was carefully 'shelled' out, the hole retapped and a replacement inserted, and this process also occurred in other places.

The erecting shop staff worked on a bonus system, payment being made after a locomotive had passed through the shop doors, so sometimes if a holiday was looming and extra cash desirable completion was effected in rather a rush. Then more faults than usual would be found on the yard steam test, although some jobs always came up after such a test, and if it was your engine you sallied forth to put things right, taking a bag of tools with you, to become acquainted with the problem of paint.

Now Gorton had had a four-road paint shop located on the wagon shops side of the shed, but two roads had been sacrificed to find room for a canteen and the other two roads appeared to be used mainly for storage. 'Painting' now largely took place in the yard. A squad of ladies would give each locomotive a perfunctory rub over with a paraffin rag, often leaving an oily residue say in the region of the lubricators, and then apply what seemed to be more like gas tar than paint, but remember that this was wartime. One coat provided the finish, and that finish took an age to dry. One of the regular painters would apply the transfers and varnish them over but one's work was never on a cab or tender side. Be on the framing and in no time at all your overalls and hands were adorned with a black sticky substance that later took some removing. Let lighting up or testing be a smoky process, and removal became even more obstinate. Often when working on an Atlantic, or an early 'Director' a hammer blow would dislodge a piece of LNER paintwork or reveal a gloriously smooth finished maroon or deep green to give you an insight as to just what care must have been taken in turning out a Great Central engine in the days of John G. but, alas, those days were now long gone.

This outside rectification work was frequently necessary after a locomotive had been through its shed test before being returned to traffic. Then you humped your tool bag over a much greater distance and hoped that you didn't need any tool you had not brought with you otherwise a second hike would be called for. However, provided the weather on such occasions was not too adverse, rectification work did provide a change from shop routine.

The erecting shop brought with it an increase in the day's physical activity. In the previous shops, boiler mounting partially excepted, you worked at a bench with your feet on the floor. Now you went from bench to locomotive going either down into a pit or up a ladder to the framing, cab or boiler top, or as an apprentice into a side tank.

These contained a series of baffles. Some ran from the bottom up, some from the top down, so you dropped in through the filler, took hold of your tools and a candle, and then did a sort of steeple chase over and under the aforementioned baffles hoping you would not drop your candle in the journey,

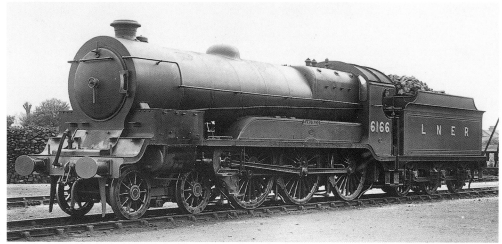

The six 'B7' (GCR '9P') class engines were Gorton's biggest express locomotives but were not over successful. They could pull and were smooth riding but heavy on coal consumption. This is No. 6166, originally named *Earl Haig*, later to be the subject of a Gorton rebuild during my time there. Here it is after an earlier spell in the erecting shop when Caprotti valve gear was fitted in late 1929.

The 20-strong members of the LNER 'L1', later 'L3', class were built at Gorton between 1914 and 1917 being the first British engines to sport the 2-6-4 wheel arrangement. They were strongly built and heavy to work on, as I found out when one came into section four for overhaul. My mate kindly giving me the job of holding boltheads in the side tanks. Powerful, but allegedly short of brake power, I met them in my footplate days again as several were then being used as bankers on the Woodhead line. I was then quite impressed by the spacious layout of the cabs, and their 'bark' when hard at work.

until you reached the far and business end. I was in the tank of a 2-6-4T '1B' or 'L1' tank when my candle fell over, and as I did not have any matches it was a lucky that I did not suffer from claustrophobia as I made my way back into the daylight to be asked by my mate why it was taking so long just to have a few bolt heads secured for tightening.

After some months on section four I was commanded to report to chargehand Worthington on section nine in three bay, for this was the so called 'new' work section. The one and only 'B3'/'9P' rebuild, No. 6166, had been completed some time earlier and a projected rebuilding of the four-cylinder 'Black Pigs' or 'B7s' had been put on hold; a circumstance I after my encounters with Nos. 1361 and 1381 much regretted. Now two jobs were in hand, namely fitting new frames to some of the 4-6-2 'A5' or '9N' tanks and turning various 'O4s', or an '8K' to use the GCR notation, into an 'O1' and at first I found myself involved in the latter activity.

My mate was a Hercules, who on arrival at work would often put on a pair of carpet slippers, fasten up his overalls to the neck, and light up a cheroot. Then he was ready to start work, and wonder here at carpet slippers in an erecting shop. He was often of uncertain temper, and whether you liked it or not, you answered not to your real name but 'Jim'. Here was another character, but as a fitter he was virtually unbeatable, whilst watching him with a file was like watching a milling machine in action and I soon had a demonstration of his capabilities.

I had a cylinder cover in a vice and using a round file was easing out two or three stud holes, as these had been drilled slightly out of line and so the cover could not be fitted to the end of the cylinder as received. Reaching my marks I stood back and whistled for the overhead crane when my mate, who was working on the other side of the engine and some way off, bounded round to tell me that I was not there to waste the company's power. When I indicated that there was no way I could lift that heavy cast-iron lump, he went to the vice, spun it open, grabbing the cover with one hand, strolled to the cylinder with it, gave it a twist of the wrist, and popped it neatly onto the studs. That I was told was the way I would do it 'Jim' in the future.

An incoming 'O4' was stripped down to the frames, and then the original cylinders were removed. Each of these were combined with the valve chest in a casting which had two flanges. The first against the cylinders was bolted to the frame, the second at the end of its steamchest bolted to the corresponding flange on the other steamchest. The complete assembly gave a very substantial frame stay effect, but when removed left a large hole in each side of the frame and the first task was to fill this with a plate of frame thickness.

This had bevelled edges, the frame was similarly chamfered, and the plate welded into place. We then had to ensure that the end result was not only flush with the original frame, but that the surface of both plate and frame were flat enough to ensure that a steam tight joint could be made. With a template the apertures that would line up with the steam ports were marked out and cut, and then the smokebox saddle was inserted between the frames, and once accurately located partially bolted in place. The centre of the driving hornway was then determined by the top corner of a straight edge running across the frames, a varnish and putty jointing compound applied to both cylinder face and the surfaced area of the frame, and then with lines and a length gauge

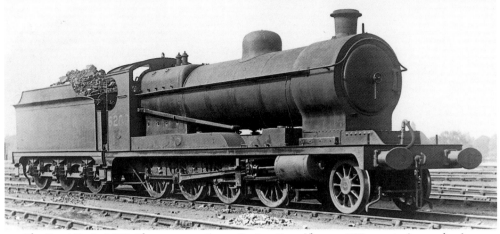

The Great Central '8K'. There were smiles on Section Four when an '8K' came in for overhaul as they were easy to work on and provided a good bonus payment. A total of 647 of these excellent engines were built and the LNER took over 131 plus 17 of the larger-boilered version, the '8M'. The LNER classified them as 'O4' for the '8K' and 'O5' for the '8M', buying many 1914-18 wartime ROD examples and completing the rebuilding of the '8Ms' to 'O4s' to give a total of 421 class members. Various examples came to be rebuilt from 1929 and I often wondered why until the 'O4/8s' came on the scene. No. 6260, here sporting a 'flower pot' chimney, was completed by the North British Locomotive Co. in October 1918 for the ROD. Purchased by the LNER in March 1924 it became No. 63833 in British Railways stock. Never the victim of any rebuilding scheme it was finally withdrawn in January 1962.

Over the years 1944 to 1958 a total of 99 engines were updated with 'B1' boilers and side window cabs, whilst crew comfort was further enhanced thanks to the provision of padded seats. These rebuilds could occur on any erecting shop section. Gorton boiler shops were prolific 'B1' boiler producers, a total of 263 being built with examples not only used in the Tank but being supplied also to the North British Locomotive Co. in Glasgow. This particular 'O4', No. 63688, is in very work-a-day condition.

secured to the frame by several temporary bolts. When my mate was satisfied that the cylinder was accurately placed I went to ask Mr Whittaker to come and check that everything was as it should be and when he had carefully checked what we had done, and pronounced himself satisfied, the work of bolting on those cylinders could begin. A driller opened out the undersized holes that had been previously machined in the casting, his drill going also through the frames, and in certain places the smokebox saddle as well. The erecting shop also had its own turner, and he would then provide a sufficient quantity of bolts that would be a tight fit in every hole. All we then had to do was to drive them home, and ensure that each and every nut was screwed up tight, very tight.

My mate used the big hammer to some effect, whilst I held the 'Dolly' and those bolts rocketed home. I tried not to think as to what would happen to me should he miss but of course he was too skilled for such to occur. Once the cylinder and smokebox saddle assemblies were in place, much of the rest of the locomotive seemed to go together quite quickly and when the boiler had been added my mate showed me how he could once again combine speed with accuracy.

The main steam pipes from the header to the cylinders passed through holes cut in the sides of the smokebox and these had to be made air tight. To make the seal we were provided with four plates for each side, each being bent to the inside radius of the smokebox. These had then to be fitted most carefully around the steam bends in such a way that two lapped together horizontally and two vertically, then when a satisfactory fit had been reached jointing compound was run in, and the whole arrangement bolted together. I had not finished my first two by the time his side was all complete and then it was a case of 'Jim, get a ****** move on'.

Below the smokebox saddle was the pony truck bearer, and when we came to put this in place I held my breath, for one of my premium friends had been so engaged with my mate on an earlier rebuild and was trying to make a point when 'Hercules' became very agitated, and told him to 'Shut up, else someone will get hurt'. My friend tried again, to be sharply silenced, so he retreated to a safe distance and called out 'I was only trying to tell you that we have got it upside down'. Fortunately we had no such problem but there were a few 'Tender' moments as we added numerous parts until all was ready for wheeling.

Eventually where once had stood an '8K'/'O4' now stood an unpainted 'O1' No. 63760, and so it came to be lifted to the bottom of the shop for painting, checking over, and its first yard steam test. Little adjustment was required and once we had finished the few necessary odd jobs it was washed out, and taken over to the running shed for another examination and then its trial trip before acceptance by the Locomotive Running Department and so being added to the working stock. Here came a bonus, as brand new or heavily rebuilt locomotives went on their first trial trip accompanied by a senior fitter, and oft-times his apprentice, so my mate and I, as honorary godparents, went along to make sure that all was well.

The usual practice on such occasions was to come off shed tender first, and then to run down to Ashburys. At that point, direction was reversed and the Romiley direct line via Reddish was followed as far as the junction there that took you via a right-hand curve down to Stockport Tiviot Dale station. The tracks round this curve had been used in earlier days by a London Road to Stockport passenger service only this former GCR operation had long since been withdrawn. Now trial trips continued along CLC tracks as far as Northwich Loco where the engine could be turned, checked over and any minor problem rectified. After a short rest for the crew the homeward journey could commence via the same route in reverse.

I was lucky enough to be allowed to take part in four such trips, three being with 'O1s' and one with an 'A5' tank engine, for section nine, as well as rebuilding 'O4s', was also engaged every now and then in reframing these big tank engines that were so much a part of the London Marylebone suburban services for so many years. One 'O1' run, though, certainly differed from the others. We set off as usual taking the Ashburys-Reddish route but this morning the CLC line was busier than ever, and signal check followed signal check until at either Northenden or Baguley (I cannot now remember which) we were put inside, and told that there was no chance of our reaching Northwich. My mate and our driver then had a conference and decided it was far to early to go back to Gorton, so we would stay where we were until around the usual hour for passing that station when heading homewards. As keen gardeners they elected to go to visit some local horticultural establishment that was not too far away leaving the fireman and I to stretch out in the hot sunshine on an adjacent grassy bank, and there we were soon fast asleep. We were awakened rather rudely with boots prodding our ribs.

The 'O1' ex-'O4' rebuilds were carried out in section nine (chargehand Worthington) starting with No. 6595 later 3795. Here one very scruffy example is reversing off Gorton shed, obvious from the position of the valve gear. This was the only part of the erecting shop in my experience where one kept reasonably clean throughout a full days work as other personnel did the stripping before section nine men started conversion, beginning with a set of frames.

An 'O1' running light and brand new out of shops did not require a huge fire and copious quantities of steam to make it go. Very little and not too often was a much better recipe so by the time we had reached what was to become our terminus there was not over much fire in the grate. Now there was a lot less, in effect none, as nothing at all had been done to it during the period of our siesta. Urgent repair work was put in hand but fortunately there was steam in the boiler, so the blower could be used to good effect, but irrespective as to what was happening in the firebox there was a hot atmosphere on the footplate and two fortunes were told in very succinct terms.

I could have enjoyed my stay on section nine but the uncertain temper of my mate often made working with him something of a trial. When in a good humour he was the nicest of men but this 'Jim' was always very wary as to what he said and did all the time he was in his company.

That time duly came to an end with my transfer to the erecting shop yard, there to join our two steam testers Arthur and Charlie. Arthur was another dyed in the wool Gorton man, but Charlie often seemed to take a different view of GCR products as he was an ex-M&GN man who tended to suggest that there was nothing like the Melton Constable workshops as they were in the days of their highly respected chief Mr Marriot. Like other men of his generation he had to start work in his earlier days not at 7.55 am, as we now did, but at 6.00 am when the local public houses would be open to serve rum and coffee to those going to work, and when there were no acetylene burners or up to date machine tools. Hand fitting meant just that, it was all heavily manual, but fitting was not now anything that I had to practice.

The day's routine really began not at starting time in the morning but immediately after lunch by which time a locomotive fresh out of the erecting shop and as yet in an unpainted (tarred) state would be fired up and close to making steam if indeed there was not already some pressure in the boiler. You armed yourself with a pencil and note book, a piece of yellow waxy 'foreman's' chalk, and a wheeltapper's long shafted hammer or, as Arthur always put it, 'a hammer with a boarding house reach'. You then started at the front buffer beam looking for missing or unopened split pins, loose nuts, unclipped pipework and any other visible fault. Each one was marked with the chalk and then entered up in the note book. You progressed down both, sides underneath, over the top of the boiler, and through the cab, and doing likewise to the tender similarly if one was fitted at this stage.

By now steam would be raised so injectors, the ejector, the other steam controls, and all the pipe work were checked both for operation and leaks, and then the locomotive was run slowly up and down the yard. In my period on yard test we did not see a repeat of the classic occasion when, thanks to the incorporation of some wrong eccentric assembly, those present saw an 'N5' tank locomotive going backwards when in forwards gear and backwards when it should have been puffing away chimney first.

A porous brick that had been well impregnated with paraffin was then set alight. This was held in a wire frame that also had a very long wire handle. You stood on the framing as the engine ran up and down the yard and ran the flame around all the smokebox joints when any area that might be drawing air was suitably marked. Then the smokebox door was opened and one did the same again around the main steam bends, and the header etc. Here I always seemed to be unlucky as by the time we reached this stage of the proceedings it was late afternoon and invariably raining, when a standard Manchester drizzle did nothing to help one's notebook entries.

The next morning after starting time you settled down in the testers cabin with its excellent view of both the main line and the shed exit, and began to write up in shop order all the faults listed the previous day. Your list went into a foolscap book but two carbon copies had also to be produced so one had to press hard on the pencil to make the bottom one legible. When the writing stint was complete and Arthur or his mate had checked the end result you went on a tour of the premises. The first copy went to the works manager's office but the other was sliced up and you then gave the various shop foremen their part of the last copy, which of course spelled out faults that involved their men or repaired components. This all took quite a time especially if a visit to the tender shop was involved, and so before you drew breath it was lunch time and the process started all over again.

There never was a day when we had nothing to test, indeed about two or occasionally three subjects a day seemed about the norm during my time in the yard. Being on this job certainly gave one an eye as to what to look for and where and in the process you saw every side of every type of locomotive that was then on the Gorton maintenance list.

When you had the chance to be involved in this sort of work one thing rapidly became obvious, namely how so much of the detail to be found in later Robinson era Great Central designs was obviously modelled on what had been done in earlier years, i.e. during the regime of Thomas Parker. I did wonder if this mechanical lineage could be traced back even further to the days of Charles Sacré, but this was something I could not discover, as by now all the products of his days at Gorton had made their last journey to the scrap yard.

Now though I was to undertake a journey, back to the Locomotive Running Department, for each of us in turn was given a period of running shed experience. Consequently one Friday evening my time wallet No. 3465 was thrown into that box in the time lodge for the last time, and in replacement I was given clock card No. 7064. A clock card? Could things in the shed really be more up to date? I was very soon to find the answer to that question, an answer that was firmly in the negative.

By now one thing had struck me. It was much easier and more pleasant if one had to work at Gorton, to do so in the machine or fitting shops, even if, say, reconditioning ejectors or eccentrics was repititous. Erecting shop work - at the same basic rate of pay - was dirty and far more physically demanding but men like my old mate Joe Bromley did it for years and were real experts. It did not matter what the job was. Anything that had to be done, stripping or erecting they could do it and do it well, but I would not have wished to think that I would have to spend my years to retirement so engaged.

Watching trains go by is one thing. Working on steam engines built 12 inches to the foot scale is quite another matter!

Chapter Eight

Basic Operations

My transfer to the shed took place in the spring, and at this point a description of what had been the Great Central's main running establishment is desirable.

An incoming locomotive arrived on the mid-1930s wet pit, where the fire was cleaned, the contents of the ash pan dropped or raked out into the quenching water, and where the smoke box was cleaned when the engine passed under the mechanical coaling plant. This was the second such to be provided by the LNER which, in combination with the wet pit, did much to ease shed operation. Once initial servicing was completed at these facilities which lay parallel to the main line the locomotive followed tracks that turned through 90 degrees, the first passing the No. 2 cabin which was where the running foremen who controlled these operations were based.

Then came cabin No. 1, a signal box-like structure but with no levers. Here another set of running foremen, who like their No. 2 confrères were ex-footplate men working on shifts round the clock, had their base. They logged in and out every engine together with any moves one might make from one road to another, so that they could provide at any time details as to what piece of motive power stood where. Behind this cabin lay some sidings and the works weigh house where the load on each axle of every overhauled unit could be weighed before the springs were adjusted and where engines awaiting works, or sadly scrap, could be stored. These areas had once been covered by the old coaling stage, when controlling yard movements must have been a sore trial.

From the No. 1 cabin the tracks fanned out, to the turntable, to two lines to the south of the shed building, where stood an outside set of shear legs, and then to the 20 roads that led into the shed itself, or rather a part of a shed. The right-hand track as one looked into the 'building' was the one that traditionally housed the breakdown crane and accident vans, then came the next nine. Then a set of brick arches formed an open style boundary wall before the next 10 tracks followed only now most of these were open to the elements, as the roof generally was in a very poor condition and had been removed from this area in the interests of safety. Each set of rails had two pits, one outside the shed where in earlier times fires had been cleaned the other pit running within the walls up to the brick floored walkway that ran right across the shed at right-angles to the 20 roads, 19 of which terminated with a low 'Stop' casting being bolted to each rail.

In the right-hand corner of the shed built onto this walkway was the wooden lean-to shed office now occupied by foreman Fred Foster who had previously been at Heaton Mersey, and prior to that one of the three Gorton shift mechanical foreman, the other two being Messrs Moreton and Topping. Mr Foster was now in charge of all mechanical repairs having a chargehand, Roland Leach, a clerk, and a chargehand cleaner to assist him.

There had been changes here, for following the tragic death of Mr Ivors who had previously run Gorton Shed, there was now an assistant district locomotive

The erecting shop. This is two bay, section six. In the foreground is a 'J39' class 0-6-0 on the stripping side about to be dismantled. There is strangely a vacant space on the building side, so an overhauled locomotive must recently have vacated the area and been carried by the overhead cranes to the end of the shop for its yard inspection and steam test.

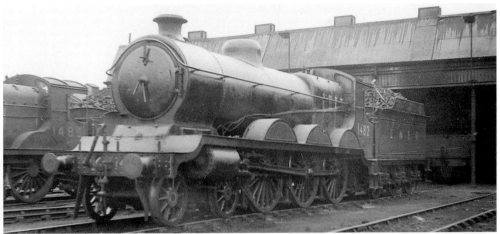

After the war had ended the Directors of the LNER decided to brighten up travel and so decreed that all locomotives were to be painted green. Some paint shops were quick off the mark but the half left of the Gorton establishment was not (the other two roads had become a canteen). One ex-GCR engine, 'B4' class 4-6-0 *Immingham* now No. 1482, formerly No. 6097, did receive the fully-lined treatment in 1946 and was then allocated to Ardsley. The last survivor of a once 10-strong class, *Immingham* was withdrawn in November 1950.

A total of 289 'J39' class 0-6-0s were built between 1926 and 1941. They were regarded as standard engines but there were different brake arrangements, different injectors, different lubricators and different regulators between them - so much for standardisation. Gorton in my shed days had around 18 on allocation that were frequently to be found on the wheel drop. Our drivers regarded them as powerful engines but the fitters felt that the driving axle boxes were not up to the piston loading imposed on them. Here we see No. 1275 on shed at Lincoln on 17th May, 1932.   *T.G. Hepburn/Rail Archive Stephenson*

As mentioned in the text the last four 'V2' class 2-6-2 locomotives were amended by Edward Thompson and became class 'A2' 4-6-2s. One example was allocated to Gorton and ran trials on London trains during my yard steam test days. I often saw it passing our testers cabin whilst working on that section. It seemed to be an impressive locomotive but, alas, this was not a highly successful design.

Another section nine job in my days was to fit new frames to some of the 'A5' class tank locomotives that for years monopolised the suburban services out of London Marylebone. Here one such locomotive, a GCR '9N' class, tank pulls out of Marylebone. Between 1911 and 1917 Gorton turned out 21 of these locomotives. Ten more with side window cabs followed in 1923. Thirteen more came in 1925/26 from Hawthorn, Leslie for the former North Eastern Railway area.

superintendent and a shedmaster as well, this latter post being filled by Mr Robinson who had been moved over from Northwich. Next to the office in the back wall was a door leading to a small yard and then a line of benches led to a large door giving access to the fitting shop, and through this door ran the one set of rails that did not end as previously described.

At the office end of the benches could be found the 'handy men' who spent their days fitting brake shoes and adjusting the same, then at the other end was the section used by the running fitters who worked alternate day and night shifts, numbering around 12 in total. After completing some task or other these men would return to their section of bench to find any notes left by Leach which would detail what new jobs awaited them.

Inside the fitting shop were a wheel lathe at the end of those rails, and two other lathes, one large and one smaller, worked by 'Happy' Hopkinson (who was not noted for a smiling countenance) on the larger one and Benny Hill on the smaller. Benny, a delightful character, was a keen Manchester City fan. If his team had lost on Saturday, he would, until around Wednesday, tell all and sundry how they should have won, but from then onwards optimism would replace gloom and next Saturday there would be a positive result certain - or so he would forecast. The fitting shop was also home to the specialists who dealt mainly with injectors, ejectors and lubrication, plus the 'stayers' who worked on days and undertook valve and piston examinations or the bigger jobs that came in, or worked the wheel drop or on the two internal shear legs to be found near the head of the tracks that lay on either side of that internal arched wall.

Further along the back wall were the boilermakers quarters, and the section used by the two brick-archmen, whilst the three end unroofed lines usually provided space for engines newly off works. After the running department trial trip drivers produced their list of any noted faults the shopmen would effect the sort of rectification previously mentioned. Finally three examining fitters looked over every engine that came on shed and so found more subjects for chargehand Leach to write on those fitters notes. A squad of shed labourers, shed enginemen, cleaners, and last but by no means least the coppersmith, completed the workforce to ensure that Gorton's 170 or so locomotives were kept operational, for Gorton was certainly in the first division of LNER establishments. It was therefore into this world that I was now posted, and my various visits from the top office had given me no inkling at all as to what it would be like to be, as it were, at the 'coalface'.

The first job I was given was to produce some drawings showing the difference between what the profiles of the wheels of a 'V2' were and what they ought to have been. The flanges were certainly very thin, so a few days later that 'V2' disappeared towards Doncaster, and did not return. Then I was told to work with running repair fitter Herbert Hill, a move which saw the beginning of a friendship that lasted from that day over a period of just 50 years, until he passed away in May 1998 at 93 years of age.

Our work mainly consisted of repairing leaking pipes, rectifying blowing glands, cleaning out clogged sand boxes and the job I detested, namely securing the top back slide bar bolts on our complement of around 24 'C13' local tank locomotives. These had a hard life, wear being accentuated by all the stopping

During this period the end of the Oldham trams came with the delivery of 14 Leyland 'PD1'/Roe-bodied 7 ft 6 in. wide double-deckers, Nos. 228 to 241. They were built to standards much better than those contained in the wartime utility specification and so had upholstered seats but sadly lacked heaters. The very first 'PD1' chassis, PD1/460652 was delivered to the City Coach Company on 19th March, 1946, the last, PD1/510766 on 14th September, 1951 to Central SMT. Just 1,950 chassis of this type were produced.

The 14 tramway replacement 7 ft 6 in. wide Leyland 'PD1s' of 1946, Nos. 228 to 241 were not quite up to Oldham's normal standard, but still a big improvement on the wartime utility bus. This view of the lower saloon of No. 235 shows that no heater adorns the front bulkhead and that leather has replaced the usual seating moquette.

and starting they had to do on their numerous Hadfield, Hayfield, Macclesfield and Oldham or Stalybridge journeys. On running work you were seldom still. You moved from track to track with periodic returns to your strip of bench to see what chargehand Leach had in store for you, and began to wish you had the flexibility of a snake and fingers that were burn proof.

Often you were struggling to complete a job on an engine when it was due to go off shed and the driver or a mechanical foreman would be urging you to greater efforts, but at least this was springtime and the weather was largely favourable. I was to find out about winter later. After a few days Herbert went onto nights so I then worked with other running repair men until I was put with Arthur who was the regular wheel drop fitter, and here was a new experience.

I should think that half our subjects were 'J39s' so what did we do? First drop off the side rods, and position the locomotive so that the bottom of the flange of the driving wheels if it was a driving box was in line with the head of the ram. Then start the pump, driven by a long belt from an overhead shaft. If the belt slipped, tension it with the help of a broom handle and a nearby drain pipe. Up comes the ram from the floor, and lifts the wheel set above the rails this needing quite an upward force. Now undo the fish plate bolts and lift back around eight feet of rail on each side, together with the substantial timber baulks carrying those rails over the drop pit. Then pinch the wheelset round so that the big ends were in a suitable position to allow the wheels to be lowered. Let the ram down so the axleboxes rested on the horn stays. Now the load was off the springs so their pins could be knocked out. Then remove any brake rod than might prevent progress, and lift the wheels once more. Drop the horn stays, lower the ram, and down will come wheels, axleboxes, springs and big ends, bringing the pistons towards the back of the cylinders. Drop the springs, dismantle the box, and decide what needs to be done. Often remetalling the brass, and cleaning up the journal would allow completion to take place, but sometimes the journal would be badly scored. Here was a deficiency for the pit was not deep enough to allow the wheels to be kept in it as the rails were replaced, and the engine drawn over the top to release them. Consequently they had to be put back in the engine so it could be pinched up to the nearby shear legs, when with the tender disconnected and the front end sufficiently high the set could be rolled clear into the fitting shop, and to be craned onto the wheel lathe. On occasions the journals would be in such a bad state as to be transported across to the works for more drastic remedial attention, and here Gorton Shed was very fortunate in having all the extensive 'Tank' facilities so close at hand.

I had had around four months' experience in the shed, running from early March into the spring and early summer weather, but then came instructions to make yet another move, instructions that reached me one Friday lunchtime. After only a few days in the shed I had ceased to have my midday meal in the staff dining room thanks to the conditions of my overalls, but I must make it clear that working in that establishment had opened up new gastronomical vistas. There was some doubt as to whether or not we were in order in in following our new food trail, but several of us had started to gravitate to the canteen in the Ashburys goods depot, where very superior sustenance was served in what undoubtedly was a period of acute post-war food shortage. Now

'Goodbye old friends'. Saturday 3rd August, 1946 saw the end of the 27 Oldham trams that had served the town throughout the war. No. 4 is seen here in Wallshaw Depot (now demolished) after working the last journey. Mayor Stirling T. Marron (in the top hat) who did some driving stands by the front dash with the General Manager Cyril Percy Paige to his right. Twenty-one cars were broken up in the depot - six survived to be sold to Gateshead when Delph saw trams passing through.

Although Oldham Transport was firmly in favour of Leylands two batches of Crossley buses appeared in 1948. Nos. 292 to 301 were 10 Roe-bodied single-deckers whilst Nos. 302 to 311 were a further 10 vehicles with Crossley double-deck coachwork. All 20 incorporated the notorious type '7' 8.6 litre engine but thanks to the lighter weight of the single-deckers their performance came to be regarded as quite acceptable. All had Crossley constant mesh gearboxes, much easier to manipulate than that in the Leyland 'PD1'.

it might have been that this better fare resulted from the fact that a good deal of market produce came into Manchester via that precise location, but it was obviously not politic to ask any relevant questions.

On the day in question I was in the process of demolishing a bowl of best goods depot vegetable soup, when the door opened and one of our locomotive inspectors came in, looked around, spotted me, and made a bee-line for me. He then looked at what was on my plate, remarked upon how good it looked, and promptly had one brought to him, note here rank meant no queuing. He began to tuck into this and whilst so doing handed me an envelope with the words, 'Here at last are your cards'.

Well the envelope did contain a card, in the form of a footplate pass signed by the running superintendent Mr G. Musgrave himself which allowed me to travel between all Great Central section stations, only I soon began to interpret this as 'All Stations To *and* From'. With the card was a letter telling me to spend time on every sort of train from expresses to slow goods, and to vary between nights and days. I was also to be careful in the process not to damage any LNER property or myself as I journeyed about the system; obviously someone had stressed the last two items in the proper order.

I could hardly wait for Monday to dawn, and to start using yet another staff number, namely 7048.

Thanks to the outbreak of the 1939 war the intended Oldham Daimler/Gardner single-deckers never did appear. After the war, though, Oldham did receive 25 'CVD-6' double-deckers Nos. 312 to 336. All should have had Crossley bodies similar to those of Nos. 312 to 336 all-Crossley series. Errwood Park was, however, too busy to give the desired early delivery so Nos. 302 to 311 came into stock with teak-framed Roe bodies. Here is No. 314 in Rochdale new in 1948. The Crossley-bodied batch were delivered in 1949. All 25 lasted for some 15-16 years. This is a Bob Mack photograph.

Fifty Vulcan Foundry-built 'B1' class 4-6-0s, Nos. 1140 to 1189, came from Newton-le-Willows between April 1947 and the August of that year, all being delivered new via Gorton in lined green livery. Nos 1155 to 1162 became Gorton top link engines each having a regular driver. They were finished to a very high standard and were a real morale booster. I had many rides on them, No. 1162 being my favourite with No. 1155 as my number two. By the end of 1947 Gorton had an allocation of 15 'B1s'. No. 1155 lasted until March 1964 and No. 1162 for a further nine months. In this view No. 1162, now carrying its BR number, 61162, crosses the East Coast main line at Retford in July 1952.

'B1' class 4-6-0 No. 1150, of the Vulcan series, heads an express from Sheffield via Woodhead to the Manchester area and almost certainly beyond as the train is made up of LMS vehicles. Could it be a Blackpool excursion? When new these engines had SR-type identification discs. They also had the dynamo mounted at the end of the rear bogie axle.

Chapter Nine

Footplate Days

I started off quietly that first Monday morning by catching an Oldham to Guide Bridge push-and-pull train and travelling with the driver in his compartment in the ex-Great Central six-wheeled bogie leading vehicle. Then at Guide Bridge I transferred to the footplate of a 'C13' tank working to Macclesfield, seeing the route from Marple Rose Hill for the first time. I then rode back to Romiley, and had a trip on a similar locomotive 'for old times sake' through Marple, Strines, and New Mills to Hayfield, looking across the valley as we neared Strines station to our old home. I spent the rest of the day on local trains, and then finally travelled back home from Guide Bridge on the footplate of my usual 5.42 pm from that place. On Tuesday I became more venturesome, and took to the main line.

Since my 1943 trip on *Manchester City*, express motive power had undergone some changes. By 1943 all but three of the 'Footballers' had left Gorton to be replaced by a selection of 'V2s' that in the main were rostered for the very few remaining London trains, but these had been supplemented in my works yard test time by one of the four intended 'V2s' that had been modified under Edward Thompson, and turned out from Darlington as class 'A2/1' 4-6-2 Pacifics. I often saw No. 3697, later to be named *Duke of Rothesay*, as it passed me during its trial period and, even with its well set back cylinders to allow the fitting of standard connecting rods, I thought it looked quite an impressive machine. But its trials on the GC section did not reveal the problems that became manifest with the design later in its existence. Tommy Adams was often to be seen on the footplate, but regrettably I was never able to have a ride with him.

Another and perhaps more momentous change was now taking place. The Vulcan Foundry was in the process of turning out a series of 50 'B1' class 4-6-0s numbered from 1140 to 1189 and of these numbers 1155 to 1162 inclusive were allocated to Gorton and placed in the hands of the top link drivers becoming, as far as was possible, their regular engines. Consequently Dick Ball as the senior man received No. 1155, and the rest were placed similarly in seniority order down to 1162 which became Arthur Jamison's regular mount.

The other 42 examples also came to Gorton after completion at Newton-le-Willows, coming via the LMS and Ordsall Lane to receive a shed examination before being posted away to their respective homes, and what a morale booster they came to be. Finished to peacetime standards in lined-out apple green, with maroon paint inside the frames, polished and varnished pipework inside the cab and electric lighting they stood out against the hard worked occupants of Gorton Shed, and were soon to be found on virtually all of the normal express workings.

By now too the 8.25 am from London Road no longer ran to Doncaster stopping at Guide Bridge, Godley, Dinting, Hadfield, Penistone, Sheffield, Mexborough and Conisborough in the process but had been retimed to become the 8.25 am to London Marylebone. The 9.45 am to that same terminus that had continued throughout the war was also retained, and both of these trains were worked by Gorton men as far as Leicester Central.

I did not now often use the Oldham to Guide Bridge trains as I had obtained a motorcycle which was to prove almost indispensable whilst footplating. I used this to take me to the shed for 7.30 am so I could join the locomotive scheduled to take the 8.25 am out from London Road. As a result I met Arthur Jamison and his fireman Frank Henshall with whom I was to cover a good many miles in the next few months on No. 1162 which was our steed that morning.

We ran tender first to London Road with a goodly quantity of coal in the firebox, and coupled up to the waiting coaches. Our brand new green-liveried engine quite outshone every black LMS machine in the vicinity. With the 'right away' given No. 1162 pulled out and as soon as Arthur had notched up, Frank darted the fire and Ardwick vanished in a pall of black smoke, but this soon cleared to a mustard colour and Frank pointing it out to me specially said, 'When you see that, you know you are making steam!' Then with the exhaust injector on it was a case of firing continually to Guide Bridge our first stop; here the right-hand American injector was put on to prevent blowing off.

We left on time and then it was round after round as we climbed up to Woodhead, but by Hyde Junction I had been presented with the shovel and told to 'Have a go'. Fortunately No. 1162 rode very well, and I did not miss the rather narrow LNER standard fire door trap too often as Frank told me where to try to put the coal, but throwing it initially as far as the front tubeplate was not at all easy. When things became difficult as they did my teacher took over, to do so again as we approached Woodhead tunnel putting enough on to take us through the bore. Then he looked out for the distant signal as due to the curvature of the line this was not readily visible to Arthur. As soon as he saw that it was 'off' he advised his mate with a shake of the hand which Arthur acknowledged similarly and not many seconds later we plunged into the bore, the first time I had travelled through it in the up direction.

At this period it was almost impossible to put any more trains through the tunnel, so heavy was the traffic, so it goes without saying that the atmosphere was truly thick. For about 4½ minutes thick coils of smoke swirled round the cab being illuminated by the glow of the fire but No. 1162 plugged on, never giving a slip, and then we broke into daylight for an easy run down to Penistone.

From there to Sheffield the ride was so very different from that on No. 2871, this was positively enjoyable, and so in the time allowed we reached Victoria station where the bag was put in and the tender tank replenished. Our next stop was Staveley Town so I tried my hand at firing again until we were almost at that station. Here there was a local hazard. In front of you was the eight mile-long bank leading to Pilsley with an incline of 1 in 100 so steam needed, but at the London end of this station was a very wide overbridge. If the locomotive stood under it, and then blew off the crew suffered both noise and a steam bath, whilst it was not easy for the driver to see the starting signal so care in coping with the problem was very desirable. We made a clean start, breasted the rise, and then seemed to have an easy run to Annesley where Frank pointed out the shed, and then began the descent into Nottingham Victoria through the tunnels and the remains of Carrington station.

More water went into the tender at Victoria, and then followed the dash to Loughborough and Leicester. Speed now reached an all time high on our trip and I found keeping steam up to be more difficult than at any other time, Frank said I needed a lot more practice.

We duly reached Leicester on time at 12.13, were uncoupled and backed onto the turntable at the London end of the station, then the tank was again filled with water. Here was a nuisance as the parachute column valve was opened by pulling a chain downwards, but when you let that chain go the flow ceased, so you stood on the tender top, holding it down whilst gallon after gallon went into the tank. If it was raining hard this was a trial but as I did the pulling I was able to see the Leicester City Transport tramcars passing each way along Great Central Street below, never for a second realising that some day my name would be written on the flanks of their successors. With coal pushed forwards, and the fire cleaned we moved to the down end of the station to await our 12.59 pm departure, and then my two mates gave me more information about the trains we were working.

Changing engines took the minimum of time, and then we were on our way crossing over Abbey Park Road, an address I was also to know in later years, with its then reserved track tramway, to climb up through Birstall and so over Swithland reservoir to Loughborough and Nottingham. Another climb followed after we left Nottingham up towards Annesley, and then ensued a fast run down to Staveley Town for a 1.43 pm departure and after that a Sheffield arrival at 2.03 pm. Then it was another continuous bout of firing to Penistone and from there to Dunford Bridge, to roll downhill through the tunnel, clear by comparison to the up line bore, then down past Hadfield and Guide Bridge to London Road for a 3.30 pm arrival, once again on time.

I do not suppose that very many passengers used the train which had left Marylebone at 10.00 am for a journey through to Manchester, but Tuesday or not there was certainly no shortage of passengers at the stations we saw. Who would have believed that morning that in all too few years the Great Central main line would be no more, but there was one portent of things to come, for as we climbed up to Penistone we passed Thurgoland where work was in progress in the construction of the new tunnel to provide room for the electric overhead. Once the stock had been drawn clear it was tender first back to Gorton to leave No. 1162 on the wet pit, to walk down to the engineman's lobby and book off after a stint of nine hours. I went home and plunged into a hot bath for stiffness was setting in amongst a variety of muscles I had not previously known existed.

The summer of 1947 proved to be very hot, and so in what was usually very good weather I travelled frequently on those London trains with all of our top link men, but one day etched itself in my memory. It was a boiling hot Saturday, and by now my firing skills had improved to a considerable extent. Not wanting to be out too late in the evening I had caught the 9.45 London which reached Nottingham at 12.19 pm to give time to catch the 10.00 down from Marylebone that left Nottingham for Manchester at 1.07 pm. The train pulled into Victoria behind the usual Gorton 'B1' but I did not know the driver. I showed my pass

This is an unusual photograph as the locomotive is about to enter Woodhead up line tunnel tender-first. It is to be hoped that the crew had a strong set of lungs as it was bad enough going through behind the protection of a spectacle plate. Going tender first would provide one with the full benefit of Woodhead's notorious atmosphere. This was a treat I never experienced or indeed ever saw.

This train of coal empties has just left Woodhead tunnel's up bore and is about to pass Dunford station. An 'O4' class 2-8-0 and a string of empties was an almost monotonous sight on this main line. Holding the train in check with only engine and van braking available was bad enough on this side of the hill but going down with a full load on the other side of Woodhead tunnel was another matter that could give the unwary a deal of excitement. The sand drags had not been installed for nothing.

and asked if I might ride with him; he did not reply but just nodded in agreement. He then left the cab, and the fireman who looked like a wrung out rag asked me if I would, or could, do some firing as he was just about all in. He added that his mate was a man of fine principle, but who would not notch up, as he maintained it led to knocking axle boxes. He had just finished telling me all this when the driver returned and we received the 'right away'.

I took up the shovel as we entered the first tunnel and awaited him giving the reversing screw a turn but instead he turned to me and with a right-hand gesture indicated that coal should be put on the fire. All the way up the 11 miles or so of 1 in 130 gradient through Annesley tunnel to Kirkby South Junction I wielded that shovel, and every time I thought there was ample fuel on the fire the driver's left-hand gave that commanding gesture. There was a little respite as we dropped down to Hucknall, but it was then back to the shovel till we reached Pilsley. At Sheffield wanting an early night or not I bade my hosts farewell and waited for the next train to Manchester, feeling more than a little limp myself. It may be that the driver had been doing what he did on purpose to test me, but if it was his normal style of driving then he displayed a very different technique to the Gorton top link men who gave their firemen a much easier time. Some of the latter gentlemen were misers when it came to putting coal on a fire telling me that every pound they saved, saved in turn a pound of their energy. The next train to arrive was a special from the east coast with a 'B7' at the head and here I had a problem.

I am naturally left-handed so firing a left-hand drive locomotive from the fireman's right-hand side came easily. Great Central engines were all right-hand drive, and firing right-handed was an art that I never really came to master.

I did though respond to the fireman's invitation to try my hand and as it was basically a case of putting the fuel under the firehole door and letting the motion of the engine do the rest. I managed to keep pressure up, till we reached Dunford Bridge but this 'Black Pig' appeared to need almost as much coal as my previous subject. On the credit side though the riding was free from the roughness and rattles of No. 2871 or 'K3s', etc.

Now I was told that a fair proportion of my time had to be spent either on nights, or on goods trains, or both, so I tried an empty coal train or two heading from the Manchester area to Wath yard, but often we made little progress as we slogged up to Woodhead, usually seeing every loop in the process, but on such occasions the time spent in the tunnel seemed like an age. I also rode from the Mexborough end up the bank to Barnsley Junction known to the footplate fraternity as 'Plevna' but was never able to have a ride on the Garrett. I did see it but always on Mexborough Shed with a 'Not to be moved' notice on the buffer beam so the best I could do was to look over the footplate, and at the works underneath as it stood on the pit.

One night, though, I boarded the footplate of a 'J39' at Godley as it waited to come off the CLC line. It was a nasty night after a recent spell of fine weather being wet and by Crowden misty. Behind the locomotive was a rake of tank wagons presumably full but that was a question I did not ask. We actually received a clear road into the tunnel and had just entered it when there was a

Forty 'D9' class locomotives came into LNER stock in 1923 but by the time I gained my footplate pass in 1947 their numbers had been reduced to 27. Here one of the unlucky ones, No. 5110 *King George V* which was withdrawn in 1943, stands in Nottingham Victoria prior to 1939. In 1947 all 27 were on the Cheshire Lines with 16 at Brunswick and seven at Trafford Park.

'O4/7' class 2-8-0 No. 63860 leaves Penistone with a Manchester-bound coal train. This locomotive was fitted with the GN-type horizontal pull-out regulator.

Kenneth Field/Rail Archive Stephenson

bang and a gauge glass burst spraying hot water and steam everywhere. We retreated to the tender where the driver fished a raincoat out of the locker, put it over his head and dived into the resulting fog. He managed to turn off the cocks, and we resumed our passage towards Dunford Bridge with numerous slips from below.

We had a clear road again down towards Penistone, but then as we neared that station a distant was firmly on. The driver applied some brake, but exactly nothing happened, he tried some more and then we slid past a home displaying a red light. By this time he had whistled the guard for brake, and I was winding on the tender handbrake, but our progress downwards continued. The driver continued all the while to smoke his pipe but I now, somewhat worried, asked, 'What do we do if there is anything on the junction' to which he replied, removing his pipe for the purpose, 'Jump!'

As it so happened there was nothing going to or coming from the Huddersfield direction, and we finally came to a stand on the Barnsley Junction side of the station. We stopped again at that box where a driver/signalman conversation ensued. That over we proceeded gingerly down to Sheffield Victoria where the crew were relieved, and where the driver did tell his incoming replacement that the brake was a bit 'tender'. It was almost too interesting an experience so I gave up goods trains for that night and travelled back to Manchester on the 3.20 am from Victoria the down mail, with another Gorton crew.

Perhaps though my most exciting morning was on the CLC when I decided to try one of the Manchester Central to Liverpool Central expresses. This one had a 'D9' 4-4-0 at the head . We pulled slowly out of the station, and began to gain speed as we passed over the girder bridges so that by the time we hit the points at Throstles Nest Junction everything that could rattle or bang was doing so and the riding characteristics were far from pleasant. This continued to Irlam and then eased off as we climbed the Ship Canal bridge to start up yet again on the way down. Along Risley Moss the road bed ran dead straight ahead but the track felt like the well worn SHMD rails in the Hyde area, and this locomotive I did not want to fire. We hit the points at Padgate as we swung round to the left and so came to a stand in Warrington, where I did wonder if I should evacuate, but sterner thoughts prevailed.

From Warrington to Farnworth was not too bad, but then came the dive down into Liverpool Central and a stop there which was not as per book for we hit the buffer stops with a definite thump. The driver a Brunswick man asked me with a grin what I thought about 'D9s' and CLC express work. My answer was as diplomatic as possible, but should have been 'Not a lot!' I had a cup of tea and joined the crew of yet another 'D9' at the front of the next Manchester express. Given the 'right away' we set off into a very smoky tunnel and then slipped almost to a stand, when the driver suddenly left the footplate. The fireman grabbed hold of the regulator, I worked the sands, and after what seemed an age we came to a halt in the open air. The driver coughing came up the track, climbed onto the footplate and said, 'Thanks mates, that smoke kills me'. With that we set off once more and did the usual CLC dash back to Manchester, when I decided that we had a lot to be thankful for at Gorton with that fleet of brand new 'B1s'.

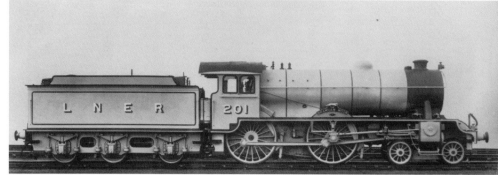

In 1939 I purchased a Hornby 'D49' 'Hunt' class clockwork engine for £1 8s. 6d. plus 7s. 6d. for the tender, and often wondered thereafter what it would be like to travel on the real No. 201 *Braham Moor*. In 1947 I did, and was disappointed. The cab was very cramped and the riding decidedly rough. There were 76 members in the class, all built at Darlington. Twenty-eight part 1 engines had piston valves, six had an original form of Caprotti gear fitted that was not a success so piston valves were substituted, the remainder had a later form of Caprotti gear including No. 201, built in 1932 and scrapped as No. 62736 in June 1958. One, No. 365 *The Morpeth,* was fitted with two inside cylinders in 1942 but was far from ideal and only lasted 10 years in that form.   *Rail Archive Stephenson*

The 70 'B16' locomotives were the North Eastern Railway's 'Black Pig' counterpart. With three cylinders and three sets of Stephenson's gear inside the frames their shed fitters must have had their moments. Seven were rebuilt by Gresley and another 17 by Thompson, but these I knew not. The ones I did ride on were as originally constructed but being GCR biased I was not very impressed. They were, though, well regarded in their home territory. One was lost in a wartime air raid. They sometimes came onto Gorton Shed after working a goods train into the area, but such visits were far from common in my time.   *J.N. Hall/Rail Archive Stephenson*

There were other locomotives about that were not in the same league, as I found out on a trip to Grimsby. This took place on an ex-Great Northern Atlantic that was nearing the end of its days. Now I know that they had a good reputation, but to me the footplate arrangements seemed primitive in the extreme, and I wondered why anyone had approved the fitting of that GN horizontal pull-out regulator that did nothing to make steam supply control easy, a design which had appeared at Gorton on reboilered 'O4s', the majority of which became known as 'O4/7s'.

Another disappointment was a trip on a 'Hunt' class 'D49' 4-4-0 from Doncaster to York. The pride of my model railway in earlier days had been a Hornby *Braham Moor*, and I had often wondered how it, and its fellows, performed in real life. As it was the cab on my example was decidedly cramped, and the riding was nearly as rough as *Manchester City* of 1943 fame.

As I said earlier I took the wording on my footplate pass rather liberally, and so I had some runs from Doncaster north as far as Newcastle, and as far south as Peterborough. The crews I travelled with showed me how to slip coal into the back corners of those wide Pacific fireboxes, and how to manipulate the water pick-up apparatus. This was easy to lower, but pulling up the scoop called for some strength as I found out one day when with a Gateshead driver called Nixon. I was rather slow in bringing the scoop out, when a torrent of water poured out of the tender filler to the amusement of my companions.

My longest day took place one Saturday. I had become friends with a Darnall driver and his mate who were booked that day to work from Sheffield a Manchester Central to Scarborough holiday express. I picked up the train which was headed by a 'B1' at Guide Bridge, but the fireman turned out to be a cleaner much younger than I who had not previously been out on the main line, so at the request of the driver, and with his concurrence I did the necessary to Sheffield where Eric and his mate were waiting, but there the 'B1' was taken off, and a 'K3' 2-6-0 put on in its place. We left to be routed via the Swinton and Knottingley line to South Milford and then took the curve into Selby. We passed through the station and then forked off to the left to go past Market Weighton and Driffield to arrive at our first stop Bridlington. This was new territory to me, but the ride stuck in my mind for as we climbed up through Bubwith to reach the summit of the wolds, I climbed over the tender front to help push some coal forwards, as the tender was not as well stocked as it might have been. Then from Bridlington we stopped at Filey and Seamer and then rolled into one of the Scarborough platforms. My friends suggested that I go back later with them, an invitation I came later to regret declining, but there was a train almost ready to leave for Hull, with a 'B16' at the head, so I rode on its rather cramped footplate to Hull only the second time I had seen that station.

From Hull it was back to Doncaster on another 'Hunt', that was just as rough as the first one, and then I was diverted, for standing in the main platform road was a London express headed by the unique 4-6-4 streamliner No. 10000. I decided that I could not miss the chance of a ride on this locomotive, finally leaving it after a most enjoyable trip at Peterborough. Then it was back to Doncaster on an 'A3' with a chance to try my hand again at firing a boiler with

No. 10000 was responsible for my longest footplating day. I saw it when I arrived in Doncaster station during the afternoon of Saturday 5th July, 1947 and could not resist having a ride on it even though its train was scheduled as first stop Peterborough.

Rail Archive Stephenson

a wide firebox, and then I rode back to Guide Bridge on another 'B1'-powered relief train that travelled to Penistone via the Barnsley line.

At Guide Bridge I mounted the awaiting motorcycle but still had enough energy left to arrive late at the dance at the Oldham bus garage that I had always meant to attend. Dance , at a bus garage? Yes, this one has a very fine hall with what in those days was a proper dance floor.

One day I went to Lincoln travelling on the 9.00 am from London Road, another Gorton working, and then transferred to an ex-Great Northern 'C12' 4-4-2 tank that was supposed to reach Chesterfield by the old Lancashire, Derbyshire & East Coast Railway, but there was a problem with Scarcliffe tunnel, so the passengers and I (not many of the former) had to detrain at the station there and board a waiting East Midlands single-deck bus, which deposited us outside the front door of Chesterfield Market Place station. Needless to say there was no convenient train from the GCR station to Sheffield, so I took an LMS train to that place, and came home via my usual route to have a trick played on me.

Messrs Jamison and Henshall came in with No. 1162, and as usual invited me to have a ride with them. I accepted, and they then kept me occupied until we received the 'right away'. Then Frank handed me the shovel and said it was all mine to Manchester. From then on I struggled. Keeping pressure up was far from easy that hot afternoon, and as I perspired my travelling companions commented amongst themselves that my associations with their Great Northern and North Eastern counterparts had not done me a lot of good so it was high time I rode more with them and had further instruction. The penny did not drop when we failed to make a clean start from Penistone, but at last we reached Dunford and entered the tunnel and of course the downhill run to home.

As we came out into the sunshine Frank courteously rose, wiped his seat, bowed and suggested I take it. He suggested that I might count the coaches behind us. It was only then that I found that whilst they had kept me occupied at Sheffield several more had been added to the rear of the train. I believe we had 14 on instead of the usual nine or ten.

There were no such problems the day I went again for another rocking run over the CLC to Liverpool, took a Mersey electric to Bidston and then rode to Wrexham on a 'C13' tank via Harwarden Bridge. Then to save time I caught a Great Western train to Chester not chancing a footplate ride, and returned to Manchester from Northgate and the CLC via Northwich to Manchester Central which from an excitement point of view was very different from a 'D9' which we had on a Liverpool fast. Having a footplate pass with the ability to roam the rails almost at will was pure joy, and what was surprising was the way in which the regular crews made you feel at home with them. Only on about two occasions did I meet any surliness, often instead when you were known the fireman would elect to take a ride in the train and leave you to do the work on your own. This was certainly a mark of confidence, but one night I did begin to wonder if confidence was not stretched just a little too far.

I boarded the footplate of a Great Central locomotive at Doncaster when the fireman immediately asked me if I could manage it. When I said 'Yes' he vanished towards the first carriage leaving me with his mate. We chugged out of the station and round the bend past St James when I picked up the shovel and put some fuel on the fire. The driver watched me and then said, 'She will do now, come over this side'. I took his place on the seat when he took off his overalls, filled a bucket from the slacker pipe with hot water and began to have a monumental wash. He then changed his trousers as I kept a wary eye on the signals for by now we were through Warmsworth cutting and heading down towards Conisborough. We passed through that station and I began to feel nervous. Here was a train with coaches and real people. A platform looks very short from a locomotive cab as you approach it, and I was not now trying my hand on the regulator of a light engine with a friendly driver behind me to make sure I did nothing wrong. My fears were eased when a now very smart individual took over again thanking me as he did so. He was he said going to take part in some panel games (whatever they were) at his club, and did not want to be late hence the ablutions, but if a signal *en route* had been on, or I had missed one then the results could have been rather too exciting.

I was lucky that summer. The 'B1' fleet, eventually to number 410 locomotives, was coming on stream and there were by now over a hundred in service, but many of the pre-Grouping designs remained, engines that by the next summer would largely have vanished to the scrapyards so I was still able to sample them worn out or not. Unfortunately, all good things have to come to an end and I came to earth with a bump at the end of September when my next job move was scheduled to take place.

After their footplate period premium apprentices usually went back to the works to some job or other but I asked if I could stay in the running department. Permission was forthcoming so now being over 21 years old I returned to Gorton Shed and fitting. But from 21 to 22 you were then regarded as being an improver so you had to wait for the 12 months to elapse before receiving the full skilled rate of pay. This did not quite mean the end of my footplate trips. I made quite a few more over the time I remained at Gorton but my very last steam ride of all was on a piece of railway I had often used in the past as a passenger.

By October 1966 steam-hauled passenger trains were becoming rather a rarity, but one which remained was the 3.35 pm from Bradford to Stockport via Halifax, Huddersfield and the Standedge tunnel. This train arrived in Stockport at 5.19 pm and returned to Bradford at 7.35 pm after making a connection at Stockport with a train from the West of England, a facility that I had also used in my Plymouth days (*see Volume Two*). Early in October it was announced that the train was to be withdrawn so I asked Eric Dalton, then British Rail's divisional manager at Leeds and Chairman of the Halifax Joint Omnibus Committee, if I could have a trip on the footplate before the end came. The answer was 'Yes', and he kindly made the necessary arrangements.

Consequently on Monday 31st October I travelled to Bradford Exchange station, and walked down the platform past about four coaches and a sausage van to find at the head Fairburn tank locomotive No. 42116 and with it awaiting my arrival the driver, fireman and a locomotive inspector. After we had left the station I took out my camera and began taking some photographs when I could almost hear my travelling companions thinking to themselves, 'We have another one here'. I ran out of film after Halifax, but looked out on a grey evening until we were approaching Huddersfield when I asked the Inspector if I could try my hand at putting some coal on the fire, adding that it would be something to tell my grandchildren about in later years, not that I then had any!

A conference followed when it was agreed that at Huddersfield the fireman would take a ride in the train, the inspector would drive, and the driver would stand by to take over his mate's job as soon as I tired, when the thought seemed to hang on the air that this would be very soon. The change round took place in Huddersfield station, I took hold of the shovel, and innocently asked what should I do and when? The inspector replied 'When I have notched up', so I gently asked what did that mean? His reply was that it was rather technical but he would tell me when the time came. We passed through the tunnel, over Springwood Junction, through the second bore, and then he said 'Right, try it now!', but the biter was about to be badly bitten.

I took up a shovel full of coal and slipped it into the back left-hand corner of the firebox, and when I had done so the inspector looking at me curiously said 'Do that again'. I asked, 'What?', and he replied, 'What you just did'. I then slipped a shovelful into the right-hand side and my cover was well and truly blown. 'Who', he asked, 'do you think you are kidding? You have fired engines before, and on the Eastern Region too, so just where did you fire Pacifics and 'V2s'? I did the firing to Stockport, and had to remark later that travelling through a level Standedge tunnel was much more pleasant than passing through the up bore of Woodhead.

We, or certainly I, had a most enjoyable evening, going onto Stockport Loco to turn the engine, and chatting about railways and engines all the time for I was with two more enthusiasts, who had had years of experience. I finally left them thinking that I could not have had a nicer way in which to say goodbye to main line steam. Here I did earlier have a trip on a Manchester to Sheffield electric, and later still on a diesel or two on the Leicester to London line but somehow it wasn't quite the same. Another reminder of that evening exists on my railway in the shape of a DJH model of a Fairburn 2-6-4 tank engine No. 42116.

Chapter Ten

Goodbye Gorton

Back now as an 'improver' I started off on running work but due to technical school commitments, worked only on days. For the next few weeks I dealt with the usual jobs that came one's way, only these came the way of the running fitters in considerable numbers. Often you would return to your part of that top of the shed bench to find a wad of chargehand Leach's notes weighted down by an old nut, and to do all the tasks then recorded would take far more than the hours remaining on the shift. It was then a case of going to look at the contents of every note, and making sure in so far as you could that there was nothing that was potentially dangerous.

Blowing glands, leaking pipes, loose bolts, broken springs, seized controls, a relay lever fitted to the rear of a side tank was one that springs to mind and big end bearings formed the usual diet with a smokebox job if you were unlucky. You could be unlucky with a big end bearing to take up if the two bolts passing through the rod and strap were tight, and then having set the crank, usually by pinching, on the best angle, slogging away with a big hammer was the only method available. In the end they always did come out, but there were those that really took some moving. When the bolts were out, you pushed the connecting rod forward, and with help lifted it, and then put a short tommy bar under it, and across the slide bars so that it was out of the way, then you could dismantle the big end by knocking out the wedge and so proceed with the next part of the operation.

A big end with say $\frac{1}{4}$ inch play was not uncommon, so one then put a straight edge across the two mating surfaces of each half brass in turn, and measured the distance from the underside of the straight edge to the inside of the bearing radius. One dimension would be greater than the other, so taking the larger half with a fitter's hammer, a sharp chisel and a file you took around $\frac{1}{8}$ in. off those two flat mating surfaces. New lubrication felts would be fitted to each brass, the oilways checked for clearance, and the big end could be then built up, but here if you had reduced the knock by $\frac{1}{8}$ in. you had to remember to place a $\frac{1}{16}$ in. liner between the back of the rear brass, and the front of the connecting rod strap so as to return the centre distance between the gudgeon pin and the crank to what it had been previously.

I then had a spell on lubricators but on looking back after some bus experience I realised that we could have been a lot more effective than we were. What we should have had was a list of every Gorton engine hung up over the bench which detailed the type of lubricator fitted, and when it had last had attention. The ones which saw the wheel drops most frequently e.g. the 'J39s' should have had their lubricators, check valves and all the associated piping checked on a regular basis, say once a week, whether we had a fault report or not. Additionally it would have been useful to have known how much oil each engine was actually using, and established on those with mechanical lubricators what was the optimum setting of the ratchet so that there was sufficient

A panoramic view of Gorton Shed when it had a roof over all 20 stabling roads. The line of arches at the centre of the building lay in front of the photographer hence the wide spacing between Nos. 10 and 11 roads in the foreground.

lubrication along with minimal usage. Setting hydrostatic lubricators would not have been easy as each individual feed was controlled by a valve readily accessible to the members of the crew, but perhaps we could have devised something that would have done the job.

Lubricator work, whilst quite light compared to most shed jobs did not suit me. The oil with which my hands were so often coated began to give me trouble and I had to pay frequent visits to the Manchester Skin Hospital and follow a rigorous course of treatment.

By this time the shed was becoming more ruinous than ever, and winter was beginning to set in. The winter of 1946/47 was the worst in living memory, and the railway and its staff suffered. What it must have been like as a shunter at, say, Dunford Bridge beggars belief. Now 1947/48 was trying to be as bad.

Still more of the roof had been removed, and with the roof had gone the electric lighting, although this was never to floodlighting proportions. Illumination consequently was again by either candle or paraffin flare, and all this taught me when I did come to have some authority over bus garage working conditions and tools that money spent in these areas was well spent.

The normal attire for a fitter at these times was two pairs of overalls, and a pair of gum boots. Your labourer would go to an engine in steam, place a wad of cotton waste on a shovel, and place the shovel in the fire until the waste began to char. Then he would rush back to you and you stuffed the wad inside your overalls, when you had for a time some inside heat and a female film star figure. When it cooled down the exercise was repeated. The boots were needed because many of the pit side drains were blocked, and the cast-iron covers over them broken, so often you had to paddle around in a few inches of water and you tried not to drop your tools into it.

All this made you think that perhaps it would have been better if you had gone back to the erecting shop like most of your confrères. But you stuck it out trusting that better weather would come, as indeed it did but not until the middle of March. Plans were afoot to rebuild the structure and provide a closed-in repair shop, but the arrival of the builders did nothing in the short term to ease what were atrocious working conditions. Amazing as it seemed later it was all accepted as fact and the staff worked on always cold and quite often wet. It was at these times that steam seemed to have little lure.

I now had further spells with Arthur on the wheel drop and then moved onto valve and piston examinations. Our main subjects turned out to be various members of the 'B7' 'Black Pig' engines as all 38 of the class were at this time allocated to Gorton. We stripped the front end down, fitting new piston rings, checking the valves, taking up the inside big ends and having the outside solid bushes remetalled and rebored, and did anything else that had been reported for examination. But from time to time we had a 'C13' tank for a change and one of these gave us a considerable fright. No. 7425 was awaiting our attentions on the Monday morning; we found the whole of the front of the cylinders and frames to be covered in a yellowish treacle like oily residue, which gave our labourer a good deal of cleaning to do.

As usual off came the cylinder covers, the connecting rods were taken down, the crossheads were 'broken' and the pistons pushed forwards so that we could

The eleven 'B8' class (GCR '1A') were not often seen at Gorton unless going to or from the works. Here one stands in post-war days in a far from immaculate condition outside the shed, or rather what was left of it. I recall the that some, but not all, of this class had marine type big ends which did not make them popular with the fitters. Conditions within our air-conditioned shed can hardly be imagined now, but those of us who were in it in that vile 1947/48 winter won't ever forget. Note another burned smokebox door.

'If only.' After a few weeks in Gorton Shed on 'B7' ('9Q') class valve and piston examinations I began to regret that the scheme to rebuild these four-cylindered machines with 'B1' boilers and cylinders had not materialised, especially as we then had all 38, so it was a case of 'If only John G. Robinson had continued to build '8N' ('B6') engines. Just three were put on the rails between 1918 and 1921. With two cylinders and a layout not unlike that of an 'O4' they were quite easy to work on and very popular with their crews. No. 5416 shown here was the first built, and was scrapped in November 1947 as No. 1346.

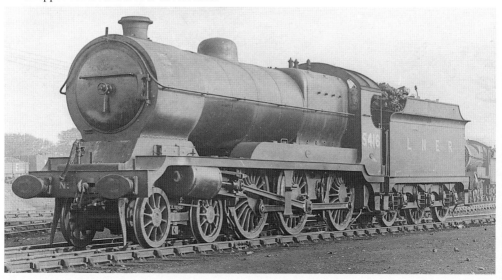

fit new rings. These came as a complete cast-iron circle. You broke this open by giving it a sharp tap with a hammer and flat chisel, and then put the ring in the cylinder after filing one of the resulting edges flat. You then overlapped the filed section over the other part of the ring after finding the place in the cylinder where there was the least wear, and made a pencil mark on the surface that faced you. You shortened the circumference of the ring to that mark, tried it in the cylinder again and then took off some more metal so that one arm of a two foot steel rule would just slide in between the gap. This gave a suitable working clearance. We also removed the slide valves, cleaned up the ports and refitted the glands also tightening up the top back slide bar bolts, a much easier job when so much had been dismantled. We completed the work late Friday afternoon, and then a fire was raised so that No. 7425 could return to duty on Saturday.

I returned to the shed on Monday morning to find my mate standing waiting for me at the gate, and he did not give me time to park the motorcycle before saying that I had to go look at No. 7425. I did and was horrified, for one cylinder cover was missing, a piston was hanging out, and the whole cylinder block was pure scrap.

As we surveyed the wreckage foreman Foster arrived on the scene, and suggested that we might have left a tool or other foreign object somewhere but being a fair-minded man he put us on our honour. We could strip the mess down but we had to tell him if we found the fault was ours. We all knew of the case where a fitter had been working in a superheater header of a 'V2' using a candle stuck as usual into a nut to keep it upright. Break came, he went off and on return the candle had burned out, but he forgot the nut and boxed up the header. The nut worked down into the cylinders and one very expensive casting of the monoblock variety was reduced to scrap; the resulting fireworks were monumental. Were we about to receive numerous rockets, or worse?

We went through our tool kits but nothing was missing nor did we find anything that might have been responsible for the damage, but even so the next few days were not happy ones. Then we were summoned to the office to be told that we were not guilty. There had, it seems, been previous problems at another shed, hence the mess at the front end, and so some instructions that should have been relayed to us never were. We breathed again, though I was then to find myself in more trouble.

The Manchester United football team was having a very good run that year, and did win the FA cup. A home team match one Saturday afternoon denuded fitter availability, so I volunteered to do some overtime to help out, not being a United fan. In the middle of my shift a driver came to me to say his sands were inoperative and he was due to work a Sheffield fast with a 'B1'. I went to look at the problem and found that three sandpipe stays, together with their pipe clips were missing, so the pipes were out of line with the rails. It was a wet afternoon, so I set about making some replacements. I cut off suitable lengths of strip steel, and then took myself into the copper shop, and livened up the smith's fire. Then I heated up the metal and bent the six pieces to shape, drilled them and bolted everything up *in situ* when one repaired engine left on time and the driver said many thanks.

During my time at Gorton around 22 'C13' tanks were allocated to the shed. Forty of these highly regarded tank engines were built between 1903 and 1905. A regular running job was to tighten up the slide bar bolts. Then towards the end of my time in the shed we began to fit new sandboxes in the back of the cab, scrapping the one behind the cab steps and converting the completed assembly to steam operation in lieu of the old gravity system. No. 5018 later became No. 7422 lasting until September 1954.

The 40 engines turned out from Darlington with the later number 1000 *Springbok* to 1039 were given names of antelope species. No. 1005 became *Bongo* and in some circles (but not Gorton) all 'B1s' were so christened. Here a spot of lubricator filling was in progress so let's hope the cylinder and axlebox oils went into the correct lubricators. Believe me this did not always happen with often unfortunate results. No. 1040, the first North British-built 'B1', also took the name *Roedeer*.

My sin was that I had strayed over a demarcation line, a being a member of the AEU since first entering the works. Alas, the representative of another union had seen me in action and made a complaint, even though none of his members would work that afternoon.

I know that Mr Foster dealt with the resulting affair as gently as he could, but it did cause me some resentment especially as I had had some recent first-hand experience as to what lack of sands on a wet and greasy rail could mean. The man who should have borne a grudge, namely our coppersmith, certainly did not and a wee while later turned out to be a real friend in need.

Right at the end of one of the roads in the roofless part of the shed stood a tank engine with all its injector pipes piled in a heap besides it, and I was told to refit the lot. These pipes had three types of securing devices, either swaged ends into which went a copper cone, the pipes being bolted together through the medium of loose three bolt flanges, or one pipe with a threaded adaptor, the other carrying a large union nut tightened up by means of a 'C' spanner, or having fixed four bolt flanges on each pipe, when you put a jointing material between the two, as you did in the second case. These pipes were of the last variety. I started off in the approved manner. Each pipe went into the vice in turn. A surface plate with marking blue was run over the jointing face of the flange and with a file I ensured that the face was as flat as possible, then the face was 'backed off'. This meant chamfering the face all round from the centre of the bolt holes to the outside edge, so that when you pulled the bolts up the flange did not 'bow' and so give an unsatisfactory seal.

Unfortunately these flanges must have had this treatment far too many times, and were decidedly thin, which was perhaps why they had been left in that pile for some time. Nevertheless I cut out the necessary Walkerite joints (here one used the ball of a hammer to do the necessary) and proceeded to sort out which went where and then to bolt them up. Steam was raised I tried the injectors, and nearly every joint sprang a leak. Needless to say chargehand Leach made some pungent comments and told me to do it all again and get it right, but the question now was, 'How?'

At this stage Bill or 'Coppernob' as we all called him hove in view having heard of my predicament. 'Take it all down', I was told, and 'cut out some more joints from rubber insertion sheet, and by the time you have done that I will be back'. He was a good as his word, and then told me to refit the piping with the rubber between each flange. Then he played the torch of his gas bottle set over each one as I tightened up the bolts, the heat plasticizing the rubber, and of course as the bolts cooled down they contracted to give an even greater pull.

When everything was cold we put the injectors on again and now there was not even a whisp anywhere. 'If you have any more trouble you know now where to come', said Bill, with a grin adding, 'Don't be in a hurry to tell Leach you have finished and be cagey about the method', only his wording was rather more basic.

Although I did not immediately realise it I was almost back where I had started for I was now spending some time down at running foremen's No. 2 cabin to see how things were organised at the coaling plant and wet pit, the latter with its ash producing propensities. Although I did not immediately recognise the fact, I was on the point of leaving Gorton almost as I had come in.

Right: The Gorton coaling plant together with adjacent wet pits was an LNER development, the whole installation greatly improving the efficiency of the shed. One task I was given was to check on the condition of the lifting gears. The view from the top was magnificent but note how the ladder was bracketed out from the sheer concrete side wall so the higher one went the more space there was beneath you, but if going up gave rise to palpitations coming down was quite another matter, as my accompanying companion discovered.

Below: An obviously hard-worked 'O4/8' class, No. 63633, stands on the tracks outside bay five of the erecting shop, awaiting entrance to the works. The sloping roof behind the locomotive indicates where the wheel shop began.
Kenneth Field/Rail Archive Stephenson

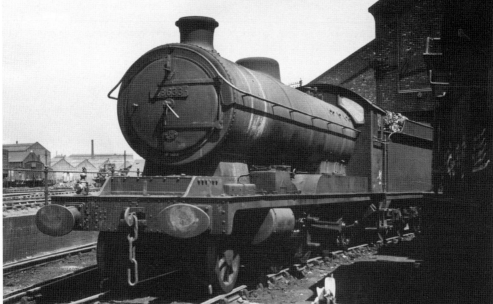

I had, though, after over 12 months as a shed fitter been seriously considering the future, and the visible facts were worthy of study. Firstly I found shedwork very heavy, whilst working conditions were to say the least abysmal. Work had commenced on rebuilding parts of the shed, and providing an enclosed workshop in the process, but even when that much needed facility was available for use, a high percentage of our workload would have to be undertaken on the running roads and on engines in steam. But how long would Gorton Shed continue as such? Work was in hand again on the pre-war electrification scheme, only a new electric shed was to be built at Reddish and there was no doubt that the fleet of locomotives it would house would be many less in number than the extensive fleet of steam engines that were based at Gorton for use on the Sheffield line.

The same sort of reasoning could also be applied to the 'Tank'. It was certainly not laid out on flow lines. True it contained a highly skilled work force, and a large number of modern machines, but these could be moved elsewhere without over much difficulty. Then one had to consider the work being done within the works. Most of this concerned normal overhauls on the still remaining ex-Great Central locomotives, and mostly were over 20 years old, whilst quite a proportion dated from the start of the century or earlier. The only stock produced under LNER auspices that came in for repair were 'J39' 0-6-0s, but these did not figure in the Thompson standard proposals. No new construction had been put in hand since before the war, but a batch of 10 'B1s' were to be built which was heartening, but another ominous factor loomed large.

The LNER was no longer in existence. We were now in the very early days of British Railways, and it was very obvious that a policy of concentration was bound to occur. The ex-Midland shed at Belle Vue was only across the tracks. I did not see it having a future, and what must happen to that establishment could easily occur to ours. It was time to go and seek a more progressive career, but despite all this reasoning, it was with very mixed feelings that I wrote out my resignation and prepared to depart. My mate of 7425 fame and I had a last week together on the valve and piston examination of 'J39' No. 4316, and I managed to have another footplate trip whilst I still had the chance.

My last Friday afternoon soon came round, when I packed up my tools, mounted my motorcycle and rode to the gate. I stopped for a last look backwards but what was then before my eyes was the strange spectacle of ex-Southern Railway 'West Country' class locomotive *Bude* being prepared to take part in its Great Central line test runs.

Actually this was not to be my final visit to Gorton, as I was to return on several more occasions including the very sad day in May 1963 when I was allowed to walk around the premises and meet many of my old tutors on the penultimate Friday before final closure. It made me feel very sorry for so many men who had worked at the 'Tank' for years, and had never imagined that redundancy would be theirs. But it made me very glad I had taken the decision to seek pastures new, for by now that earlier ambition had been realised, but that is something to be recorded later.

Going through the works was an education I would not have missed, and I honour the memory of all those with whom I came into contact in the top office,

Ex-Southern Railway 'West Country' class 4-6-2 No. 34006 *Bude* approaches Marylebone with the 8.20 am from Manchester on 9th June, 1948. Note that the engine is coupled to an ex-LMS Stanier tender.

F.R. Hebron/Rail Archive Stephenson

The construction of 'B1s' Nos. 61340 to 61349 marked a welcome return to new building at Gorton. In the immediate pre-war era Gorton was scheduled to build a series of 'J50' 0-6-0 tank engines but these were never completed. Some of the material intended for them was later taken out of storage and sent to Doncaster and fitted to those ex-Great Central 'Q4' 0-8-0 goods engines that were converted into 'Q1' shunting tanks. No. 61349 was the very last steam locomotive to be turned out new from Gorton Tank. It is seen here with a Fife Coast-Edinburgh (Waverley) stopping train at North Queensferry on 27th August, 1959.

D.T. Greenwood/Rail Archive Stephenson

or the works, or the shed, and regret that so few reminders of what once stood between Cornwall Street and Bessemer Street now exist. But if there is nothing much at 12 inches to the foot, things in '00' scale are rather different. I have at home an extensive model railway layout and amongst the perhaps overlarge stock of locomotives there are reproductions of 'B3' rebuild No. 6166, 'B7' No. 1361 (quite unforgettable), 'O1' No. 63760, whose fire was allowed to go out on its first test trip, and 'C13' tank No. 7425 whose cylinders caused us so much concern.

I did of course fully appreciate at this time of leaving that I had had two lucky breaks, firstly the LNER had not only given me my first job, but had also provided one in the Locomotive Running Department. And that in turn provided the second, when it was possible by some miracle to transfer from being a very junior clerk to premium apprentice. Now fortune was smiling again, and perhaps the luckiest break of all was mine for the taking for I was about to enter the new world of road vehicle engineering.

Some time after the works closed in May 1963 the site of Gorton Tank was almost completely cleared. When I took this photograph the joiners shop, pattern shop, foundry and brass foundry were no more. In the far centre the locomotive accountant's office block still stood as did the chief mechanical engineer's offices to the right. John G. Robinson, or latterly, G.C. Gold occupied the extreme right-hand corner of the latter building. The works site was later used for a new fruit and vegetable wholesale market. When I started early in the war such an end was totally unimaginable.

Woodstock factory. I took this photograph of the entrance to the former shadow factory in May 2002 when the premises were completely closed. The office block is on the left. The white painted gatepost on the right was where Robert Seddon was standing when I asked the gateman where I might find him.

The basis of Seddon's success was the long wheelbase (13 ft 6 in.) wagon powered by a Perkins 'P6' engine. By 1950 it had been updated with a stronger chassis, a neater radiator and bonnets and re-rated as a six-tonner. Priced in this year at £1,120 complete with spare wheel. In primer with a coach-built cab it cost £1,236 or complete with 16 ft by 7 ft 2 in. body £1,305.

The Chassis . . .

The chassis is sturdily built with frame of deep channel section braced with generous cross members. At the same time by taking extreme care to reduce unladen weight to a minimum a perfect combination of lightness and strength has been achieved.

Chapter Eleven

New Horizons

My entry into the road transport industry was basically due to the closure of the Oldham tramway system on Saturday 5th August, 1946, although it took some time before the end result as it came to affect me became apparent.

On that night the 27 surviving trams, namely 11 of the original 12 1921 vestibuled balcony cars, four of the six 1924 totally enclosed trams, and all 12 of the final 1925/6 delivery of totally enclosed cars ceased to run on the single surviving trunk route from Hollinwood through Werneth and the town centre to Waterhead. These tracks also saw the Manchester 'Pilchers' on the joint service number No. 20 that for years had terminated in Stevensons Square but which, towards the end of its days, had been extended to the edge of Piccadilly.

I decided that I ought to write the history of the system whilst those who worked on it were still around, so I wrote to Mr C.P. Paige, then the General Manager, to ask if it was possible to have access to the records. He replied that he did not feel able to help, but if I made contact with his traffic superintendent Mr S.T. Mayall he would see what he could do. I duly met Sid Mayall at his office one evening and thus began an association that would be cemented elsewhere but that was all in the future. I visited the local library whenever I could and trawled through the bound volumes of the Committee Minutes, whilst he did some research internally, but sadly quite a few stock records no longer existed having been sent for salvage during the war.

We met in his office from this time on, quite frequently, and usually after we had finished the task in hand he would take me for a stroll round the garage. It was on one such evening excursion that my attention was drawn to a most unusual bus parked in the far right-hand corner of the building. At my request we went to look at this blue and silver, rather box like, full-fronted machine, and on looking in the cab noted the maker's plate which read Seddon Diesel Vehicles, Woodstock Factory, Oldham.

Now there had been a piece in the *Oldham Evening Chronicle* a short while previously saying that the firm had taken over what had been a pre-war shadow factory where aircraft engine carburettors were made, and indeed the Corporation had taken delivery of one of the first trucks to be turned out, but buses? This was a lot more interesting!

As soon as I was home wrote a letter to the address on the plate, and a few days later a reply came telling me to contact the writer when I was next in the town. The letter was signed R.H. Seddon.

A few days later still I went into a phonebox near the Town Hall, and rang Woodstock Factory, asking for Mr Seddon. He came on the line, I gave my name, and before I could say another word he began to tear a sizeable strip off me. It was some time before I was able to point out that I was not the Hilditch he thought I was, when he apologised for the mistake, asked me where I was, and when could I present myself at his office? The answer was in about 30 minutes, so I caught the next bus to Higginshaw and then walked down the

Mk. 5 S10 Tipper
6 TON PAYLOAD

The Mk. 5S10 tipper has a wheelbase of 10ft., and has the same high quality components as the 6 ton truck. "Pilot" power operated hydraulic end tipping gear is fitted. If desired 3-way tipping gear or a two speed axle can be fitted as alternatives to the standard equipment

An almost identical but shorter 10 ft wheelbase chassis also sold very well being priced in basic form also at £1,120 or £1,322 if fitted with tipping gear (twin rams). Seddon's would of course produce a complete tipper with a 5½ cubic yard body and steel floor for £1,419 10s. and paint it in an operator's livery for an additional £35 otherwise it was supplied in grey primer.

The third member of the six ton range was the 9 ft wheelbase tractor priced at £1,170 in chassis form. With coachbuilt cab and trailer brake reaction valve the cost came out at £1,300, when Seddon's would quote for various types of trailer. The 'P6' power output was however only 79 bhp at 2,400 rpm, so too much could not be expected. All six-tonners had five-speed boxes as standard.

Mk. 5 S9/2 Tractor
8-10 TON PAYLOAD

lane to the works. On arrival I asked the gateman where I might find Mr Seddon and was surprised when he replied, 'He's theer lad', pointing to a well dressed gentleman standing by the far gatepost. I went across, introduced myself, and a visit to his office and then a tour of the works followed.

To his question, 'What do you know about road vehicles?' I had to answer nothing at all, but we talked some more, and then he made me an offer. I could start on the first possible Monday in overalls in the service department to discover all I could about Seddon trucks, and when I had been there for a sufficient time I would be transferred to the drawing office for a like spell. My pay would be £6 per week and if I was satisfactory then that could be increased. If I was not then the inevitable would ensue. Well £6 was at least a little more than Gorton then paid, and Woodstock was only about three miles from home so irrespective of any other consideration it had to be accepted.

Robert Seddon and his brother Herbert had been involved in road transport since the end of World War I, latterly running a garage in Salford. There a year or two before the start of World War II Robert had schemed out, as he once told me, on his kitchen table, a lightweight 5 ton truck powered by a Perkins P6 diesel engine, and this was first shown to the public in October 1938. Because it weighed under 2½ tons unladen it was allowed to travel at up to 30 mph, anything over that weight being legally restricted to 20 mph. It could carry up to 6 tons, and sold for the remarkable price of under £1,000 so orders were soon forthcoming and by the time the war started quite a number were on the roads, and production continued on a small scale right through to 1945.

Once peace had been restored the Seddon brothers realised that there would be an outstanding demand for new vehicles, so a lease was taken on Woodstock factory, and expansion was now very much in the air. At the time of my very first visit there was a great deal of unused space, but time would soon change that, and by the same date the original design had been updated.

There were now stronger chassis frames, improved suspension, and the original radiator once enclosed by a sheet metal surround had been replaced by a much more shapely cast aluminium unit with polished sides. Three new models had also been introduced, namely a 9 ft wheelbase tractor, a 10 ft wheelbase tipper and my bus garage sighting, a 14 ft 11 in. wheelbase bus chassis. This latter had been first shown at the 1948 Commercial Show and was priced at £1,600 plus £359 1s. 8d. purchase tax when applicable. Rather I suspect to the surprise of our Directors it had attracted some quite substantial export orders, but several home operators had purchased odd examples, and these often carried a Seddon-produced body of the type that could best be described as neat and austere. Seddon's also built the cabs, and other forms of bodywork to be found on a high proportion of their goods vehicles, having recently (at this period) opened a new body shop in a building located away from the main works which later became known as Pennine Bodies.

I found the service department or garage as it was known internally to be a refreshing change from Gorton. It was completely enclosed, and heated which was a blessing as winter was upon us. Additionally components were so much lighter than those found on railway engines, I could even walk down the shop carrying a complete set of Perkins pistons, and thereby hangs a tale. In those far

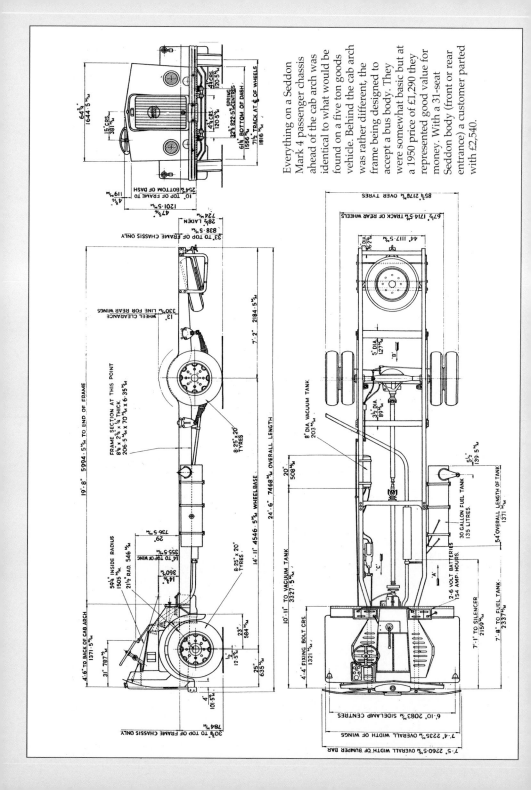

Everything on a Seddon Mark 4 passenger chassis ahead of the cab arch was identical to what would be found on a five ton goods vehicle. Behind the cab arch was rather different, the frame being designed to accept a bus body. They were somewhat basic but at a 1950 price of £1,290 they represented good value for money. With a 31-seat Seddon body (front or rear entrance) a customer parted with £2,540.

off days chromium piston rings and detergent oils were not in general use, so when an engine's oil consumption reached undesirable levels one either fitted a set of new piston rings or, if wear of the cylinders was sufficient, did a rebore and put in oversize pistons, when careful running-in was very desirable.

As a result I found myself one day being initiated into the engine reboring process. Off came the cylinder heads, the sump was dropped and the piston assemblies removed. A boring tool was then secured to the face of the cylinder block and run down each of the six bores taking out the requisite amount of material, this being a very common procedure as there was no need to go to all the trouble of taking the power unit out of the chassis. Once the boring part had been accomplished and the resulting swarf cleaned away, rebuilding followed, and in due course the engine was ready for its first restart. Now Perkins engines had an oil bath air cleaner, plus a pneumatic governor to regulate maximum revolutions by cutting off the fuel supply at the permitted level. Our apprentice was told to clean the air cleaner by washing it out with petrol, and doing likewise to the gauze element it contained, then to refit it to the engine, and of course refill it to the requisite level. Eventually he indicated that he had done the necessary and the fitter, who was teaching me how all the work was done, pressed the starter button. The engine turned over once or twice and then burst into life and more, for the air cleaner had been filled not with oil but pool petrol, and so the governor was rendered inoperable as vapour was sucked in and ignited under cylinder pressure.

That engine nearly took off. Goodness knows just how many revolutions per minute it attained but we also took off quickly as the foreman rushed out of his office, and the garage filled with smoke, but at last all the petrol was used up, and rpms died down to zero, when we reeled back to see if the cylinder heads, etc. were still in place. An inspection revealed that all was intact so another and more proper form of start was tried and normal running ensued. The following morning the owner came for his wagon, still laden with cotton bales, and took it away, being told to bring it back in a week's time when the head could be tightened down, and the tappets reset. We waited with bated breath until he returned to tell us that he did not know what we had done to his vehicle but it was 'a belter' and so better than ever.

The garage proved to be quite busy, with a string of trucks coming in for repairs. New clutch plates, replacement springs, chassis repairs and brake repairs then formed a goodly proportion of the work load, but this was all interesting stuff. I learned more than I had ever thought possible until the morning when the chief draughtsman approached me, asked if I had come on the motorcycle, and on learning that such was the case told me to go home pronto, change out of my overalls, and then report to him, as I was to start forthwith in the drawing office. This move into the drawing office, taking place as it did at virtually a moment's notice, came as quite a surprise as did another only a few days later.

I was alone in the office when the phone rang so being the only person *in situ* I went to answer it, to find Mr Robert on the other end of the line. On learning my name he told me to proceed forthwith to the Directors' dining room, knock on the door and walk in. I did as I was bid to find our four chiefs standing in a line by the fireplace. Mr Daley the first in the queue then shook me by the hand, and wished me a happy Christmas, when Mr Redmond the finance supremo

The Seddon standard bus body had metal frames and the majority were exported. Some home operators, e.g. Youngs Buses, Dallon Motor Services and Ripponden & District took very small numbers. I well recall seeing the two ordered by Bullock & Sons of Featherstone (Yorkshire) being built in 1950. Both passed with the company to the West Riding Automobile as fleet numbers 707 and 708 and Bob Mack took this photograph after the sale and repainting into West Riding's green and white livery. Bullock's had bought two earlier Seddons, fleet Nos. 334 and 335, so must have been satisfied with the new Mark 4 complete vehicle.

1950 saw the drawing office e staff busy looking on the projected three ton range. Again the range known as the Mark 7 consisted of long wheelbase (10 ft 6 in.) flat 8 ft 9 in. wheelbase tipper, or the 6 ft 10 in, wheelbase tractor. Seddons made a very smart job of designing the dash/cab layout, this example having Woodstock factory bodywork.

and Mr Herbert followed suit. Last of all was Mr Robert, who as he shook my hand, and offered his greeting also asked me how I was fairing, and then pressed a brown envelope into my palm.

I opened it later to find it contained one week's wages as a Christmas bonus, and if £6 seems a microscopic sum in current terms it was very acceptable to an impecunious youngster, who in view of his very short service could not really have ever expected such a benefit. For the record about 40 years went by after leaving Seddon's before another such bonus came my way but that is another story.

My arrival on the scene had increased the staff of the drawing office as we now had our chief Norman, plus four others, the contingent being lifted to six by the time I came to depart with one man being recruited to virtually specialize in jig and tool drawings, whilst the sixth was a junior to do the odd jobs.

One had to admire the Seddon way of doing things. We did have a machine shop but when compared to truck output this was almost minuscule. Almost every component was 'bought out'. Engines then came only from Perkins of Peterborough. Gearboxes were products of the Moss or David Brown factories, whilst axles came from Moss or Kirkstall, with two-speed units being obtained from Eaton. Frames, cross members, radiators, electrical components, castings, springs, brakes and clutches, etc. were all acquired in a similar manner, and of course fed the assembly lines so you might ask just what did we do?

The answer was quite a lot, as we were never short of work with many developments in progress. I was very interested to know just how decisions were reached to introduce a new range of vehicles but this I never did discover, perhaps it was all due to long experience in the vehicle/transport industry, but one thing was very obvious then. As the firm did not own the factory, it being rented, and not having had to spend a fortune on plant and equipment it was able to be very competitive and its products came to have a good reputation.

As for developments, Perkins had been persuaded to provide a new exhaust manifold that took the exhaust piping towards the rear of the vehicle rather than the front, and this enabled much neater bonnets to be used, although these still lacked any form of sound insulation. At the same time the pedal gear was redesigned to eliminate what had been long slots in the cab floor, Now there were two neat holes through which they passed, and these were sealed when the clutch and brake pedals were not being engaged by rubber rings.

At the same time the tractor frame was being amended to take standard Scammell coupling gear, a new 16 ft 4 in. wheelbase bus chassis to take advantage of longer permitted dimensions, and best of all a complete range of 3 ton units having Perkins P4 power units were to be introduced in 1950. All this meant that we were kept busy, but again there was much to learn. The Mark 8 Scammell-type tractor was priced in 1950 at £1,260 plus tax, whilst the initial 10 ft 6 in. 3 ton chassis was only £695, an 8 ft 9 in. wheelbase tipper then followed which complete with tipping gear came out also at £695 plus the inevitable £193 16s. 2d. purchase tax.

Then a Manchester-based dairy had the idea of purchasing a 3 ton tractor unit, and I was given the task of scheming this out around a propeller shaft that must have lain unused in the stores for quite some time. Our resident blacksmith altered a set of standard long wheelbase frames to suit this innovation, and in no time at all it was built and ready for road test, but, it was to say the least very compact, so much so that finding spaces to fit in a sufficiently sized fuel tank and a spare wheel carrier proved to be very difficult. But it worked, and so more came to be sold. This three ton range again had a very attractive Seddon coach-built cab, and also possessed flexible engine mountings which was just as well as they only had four-cylinder 50 bhp power units at 2,000 rpm, whereas the standard P6 had an output of 79 bhp at 2,400 rpm.

By now my pay had been raised to all of £8 per week so I was living well and quite enjoying life but we did have our moments. One morning I was with our chief in his partitioned-off office poring over some drawings when Mr Herbert marched in and placed a pencilled sketch over the subjects of our discussion. We had, he said, received an order for some refuse truck chassis for Holland, which in his words had to be able to negotiate 'ginnels', still no problem. It was just a case of setting back the front axle of a long wheelbase Mark V 13 ft 6 in. chassis as per sketch, and completion would be speedily effected.

At this news my chief paled, and began to point out that this was not an easy conversion. The whole of the cab structure would need to be redrawn, and available staff with all the other work in progress was precisely nil. Mr Herbert was having none of this. He indicated that a shipping date had already been promised and went on to mention rather darkly that if the vehicles did not leave the factory on time others not then named might well do so. They did, the vehicles that is, and years later when a certain large Lancashire-based concern was taking some two years to complete our bus orders I used to think of that incident, and wonder just what had gone wrong where.

Another interesting occasion was when Seddon Diesel Vehicles, for we were no longer Foster & Seddon as formerly, received an order for some vehicles to be fitted with Reo petrol engines, the first and last such to be produced. We had completed the first of these when a visit to the Reo stand at the Commercial Show revealed that they were intended to power the 16 ft 4 in. bus chassis and not the long wheelbase five ton Mark V in which at least one engine lay. Here the Seddon feature of having everything in front of the cab's rear foundation pressing being completely standard irrespective of the wheelbase dimension paid off, the substitution was quickly made, and virtually no material had to be scrapped as a result.

The whole factory was now buzzing, and it is interesting to note here that whilst several would-be manufacturers started up after the war with big plans none were to survive, whilst several well-established firms were to fail in the 1950s. Newcomers were Proctors, Rowes, Jensen (with their uniquely framed buses and truck chassis) and Motor Traction of Croydon, whilst in the latter category Sentinel, Vulcan, Tilling Stevens, Maudslay and Crossley were to cease to trade. Here I pay tribute to Messrs Robert and Herbert for their business acumen and foresight as to what the industry wanted but there was another side. My chief would tell me with a wry smile how he would take a draft order for drawing office supplies into Mr Robert. That gentleman would scrutinise it with considerable care and then strike out various items, so that only the rump could be collected from a town centre stationers by the presenter during his own lunch break. On one such occasion a dozen rubbers were struck out when, later in the afternoon, the striker came into the office to ask for the loan of such an item. When our immediate chief made a diplomatic comment as to what had transpired earlier that same day, Mr Robert gave a grin and said, 'Well you are professionals and should not need one, whereas I am only an amateur'. Some amateur!

Now the firm had not been at Woodstock factory very long, and in vehicle production terms did not have a very long history as was the case with Leyland or AEC, so our files did not contain very many drawings of outdated, or intended productions. But there was one interesting item within this range as an attempt had been made in earlier days to produce, or at least design, an oil engine with horizontally opposed pistons, something that the Rootes Group did some years later. It was an interesting project, but little was ever said about it, and no reasons were advanced for its failure to materialise.

By this time too, those monthly transport journals that I had been receiving for quite a number of years were also failing to materialise, as the member of the Transport Committee who had been passing them on to me had ceased to hold his municipal office. So I had began to buy my own, and in one issue one morning I saw an advert that caught my eye.

Leeds City Transport was seeking a senior mechanical draughtsman at a salary of £495 per annum, which from an economical point of view was not really a worthwhile proposition. £8 per week at Seddon's was worth £416 and I was living at home, and had virtually no travel expenses, so a move to Leeds would see me having to take lodgings and would make me worse off. But I wanted to be the General Manager of a municipal undertaking, and here was a job that would surely give me a start in that world. Consequently I posted off my application and hoped for the best.

All went quiet for about two weeks, and then I received an invitation to present myself for interview the following Saturday morning at the head office of the department. The end result was that on my return to Woodstock factory I submitted two weeks' notice so that I could finish the job on which I was at the time engaged, but that notice was never completed. On Tuesday morning Mr Robert came into the chief draughtsman's office, had a short chat and left, and 10 minutes later I did so too, being escorted off the premises by Norman himself. This proved to be the fate of those who were leaving to take up a post elsewhere in the transport industry, and was intended to ensure that no one could extract any sensitive drawings from the files; it was an event that gave me quite a shock.

Years later when I was a General Manager I was walking through the aisles at the Earls Court Commercial Vehicle Show when I chanced to meet Robert Seddon so I took the opportunity to thank him for taking me on, adding that without the start he gave me I would never had made any progress in the bus industry. He responded by saying that he had been annoyed when he learned that I was leaving after both time and expense had been expended on me. Giving me days off with pay to attend the Technical College was a case in point, but then he went on to say how pleased he was that I had made the approach and caused me considerable surprise by detailing some of the posts I had occupied in the subsequent years. It was a conversation that I was to look back on with pleasure for he was a man for whom I had a considerable respect and it was with great sadness that I learned of his passing in 1968.

I did wonder in later years why Seddon Atkinson trucks began to sport a large 'A' on their radiator grills, for it was the Seddon concern under Harry Redmond

Looking down the long Shaw Road assembly hall in May 2002 with the axle mounting section in the foreground. It was all very different both factory and production-wise to what one could see in the former Woodstock factory of some 50 years earlier.

Hinged-front dashes and tilt cabs were not part of Seddon vehicle specifications 50 years ago. The Oldham products of this present era were much more complicated (and expensive) than the ones I knew, looking them over made me glad I no longer had to spend my working day at a drawing board or computer screen.

that took over the much smaller, but from a products point of view, complementary Atkinson concern then based at Walton le Dale near Preston, an event that was marked by the introduction of a double circle logo to be replaced in turn by that encircled 'A'. I cannot think that the latter would have amused either Mr Robert or Mr Herbert, but after their disappearance from the firm several changes of company ownership were to occur. With the last one much worse came to transpire

In the spring of 2002 I was shocked to read in my Institution of Mechanical Engineers journal that the Oldham factory was to be closed later in the year and all production transferred to Spain of all places. So I wrote to the Managing Director to ask if I might, as a Woodstock old (very old) boy, be permitted to have a last look round before this final event took place. My request was speedily granted and so on Tuesday 28th May I was shown over the plant by Mr Richard Grey, the chief buyer and company historian, then I had a meeting with Mr Schofield the Managing Director. It was all very different to what was there in my day. The trucks themselves were so much more sophisticated, and their building took place not in the now derelict old shadow factory but in what had been the Ferranti transformer works, later to be occupied by the Seddon bus building division. But then some 54 years had elapsed since I saw that first Seddon passenger vehicle and came to a certain conclusion.

It was a nostalgic afternoon but one that was tinged with sadness, for it made me wonder just why over that span of years so much of the once extensive British commercial vehicle manufacturing capability has been allowed to vanish forever and home-built products replaced as a result by imports. This, though, is not a subject to be debated here but I must in conclusion thank Mr Schofield and Mr Grey for giving me such an interesting afternoon, and permission also to have parts of old Seddon catalogues reproduced in these pages.

Ready for delivery. A completed chassis and cab stands at the end of the Oldham works in May 2002 shortly before production began to be wound down and future build transferred to Spain. I still wonder about that circled 'A'.

Greenfield Junction, a view looking towards Oldham from a Stalybridge-Stockport train. The plating in the foreground marks the position of the former subway close by the main entrance. It was quite a walk to the Oldham line bay which was opposite the distant signal box. Rationalisation resulted in the gap in the platform canopy, but this was in the 'good old days'. Greenfield is now but a shadow of its former self. With a one minute connection time from where the train is standing to the Oldham bay meant a high speed dash along the right-hand platform.

Greenfield Junction after the lines to Oldham had been lifted. The derelict platform on the right was the 'bay' where trains from Stockport and Oldham (two coaches and an ex-LYR 0-6-0 or 2-4-2 tank) terminated. I was to come to know the place well on occasions when I travelled to and from Leeds on a daily basis. Oldham dep. 6.15, arr. Greenfield 6.30, Greenfield dep. 6.37, arr. Huddersfield 7.14, Huddersfield dep. 7.25, Leeds 8.03 am after travelling via the 'New Line' and seeing the delights of the Spen Valley. At night the 5.15 Hull-Liverpool express from Leeds arrived at Greenfield at 6.14, when, if on time, the 6.15 pm from the bay arrived in Clegg Street at 6.30 pm. This was a through train to Stockport. Then the Liverpool train was put back to 5.20 pm, 6.22 pm in Greenfield, so goodbye connection, hello bus!

Chapter Twelve

Municipal Employment

Thanks to earlier tram rides I knew just where to find the Swinegate offices of Leeds City Transport, and so turned up to find myself in the company of two other applicants and also to experience what was without doubt the most peculiar interview of my Municipal service.

We were placed initially in the private office of the Constructional Engineer, Mr Ellis, a rather slight and elderly gentleman, who was obviously not far from reaching retirement age. He asked us a few, very few, questions, until a dictaphone, on his desk gave off a continuous buzzing like the noise made by a swarm of bees. The conversation at our end at least was of very few words, and then we were given a series of instructions. If that phone or the GPO instrument rang normally we were to ignore them completely, but if the dictaphone repeated its buzzing sounds, then one of us had to pick it up and we would hear his voice telling us in turn to 'Come down'. We were then to leave the office, gain the main staircase and go to the floor below. Once there we had to turn right, proceed along the corridor and come to a door marked 'Private'. There we were to knock, and enter. After giving us these instructions the occupant of the office left and a pause of several minutes, it seemed a lot longer, followed. Then came the buzz, so, being the nearest I picked up the receiver, and proceeded to do as we had been bid.

I came to the private door knocked entered and found myself before not one man, but two. The occupant of this second and rather extensive room was obviously the senior, but no introductions were made. This new official was in his early fifties or so. He was bald with a fringe of reddish hair, and was sitting behind a very large desk with our first contact being placed to one side, and it was obvious from his speech that he hailed from north of the border. Firstly my original letter of application that lay on his desk was read with some care, and then just three questions followed these being:

1. 'Why are you looking for a position in Leeds when your home is in Oldham?'

There was no difficulty in answering that one.

2. 'If I give you a job, what will be your ultimate ambition?'

Then the light dawned. This must be Mr Findlay the former Glasgow Tramways Engineer, who had recently been installed as the Leeds General Manager, so I took a chance on this assumption being correct and replied, 'To sit, sir, in your chair'.

3. Was very unexpected. The great man turned to the Constructional Engineer, and remarked 'Well Ellis there is no lack of ambition here', when the words, 'When can you start' promptly followed, and so I was in. As I said in the previous chapter I suggested two Mondays hence, the date was agreed and so my Municipal career was about to begin. All very very strange.

Although I did not know it at this time the engineering side of the Leeds undertaking was then decidedly fragmented. Mr Ellis as Constructional Engineer having his office at headquarters was responsible for all building

The Leeds drawing office. My colleague Brian Render provided me with this view of my former workplace. My desk ran from the wall marked with an 'X'. My window (first on the left) gave me a view of Lower Briggate and City station's east end bridge. Behind me was the door to the Chief Engineer's room. Our chief draughtsman had a board facing the right-hand window, but I had the best spot, as I could easily observe all that was going on. The old office building is now an upmarket hotel!

maintenance. the repair of the tramway track, done by direct departmental labour, and ostensibly the overall control of the drawing office, but in that place we seldom were to see him. Then having equal status were firstly the redoubtable Tommy Parkinson, who as Motor Bus Engineer reigned supreme over his empire from a base at Donisthorpe Street, Mr Burbridge the Electrical Engineer, who like Mr Ellis was not far from retirement, whose staff repaired the tramway overhead and all other non-rolling stock electrical installations. Finally came Mr V. J. Matterface, the avuncular Tramways Engineer, who like Mr Ellis and Mr Burbridge had a private office in the same corridor, but who spent the greater part of his time at Kirkstall works where all the action was.

As for the drawing office, in a large room at the far end of the aforementioned corridor were to be found a chief draughtsman and seven others, three of whom were on senior grades, with one of the lesser mortals permanently outstationed at Kirkstall where he seemed to enjoy an enviable existence. Also in the same room was the desk housing the permanent way technical assistant who was to say the least a very interesting character. Here therefore was a luxury that could never be afforded by any *circa* 2000 AD transport undertaking.

My new quarters were a large desk strategically placed in one corner giving me a view of what everyone else was doing whilst they could not observe me without turning round, whilst from my window I had a view up Lower Briggate, and could easily see all the trains leaving City station for the East. The difference though work wise between this new office and the one I had just left was greater than I had known when leaving Gorton for Seddon's, and so was almost beyond belief. At Woodstock Factory there was an almost constant pressure to finish one drawing and then proceed with the next. Here you could not really say there was a quiet calm in our large abode on the second floor with its separate print room and adjacent dark room where Beeston Jack, well he was called Jack and he did live in Beeston, printed off the negatives he had taken as the department's photographer, but urgency was just about conspicuous by its absence. The chief draughtsman too could not be described as a gentleman of strong personality and firm views but £495 per annum, even if I had to pay for lodgings, and my fare home at weekends, was not to be sneezed at, if one took future possibilities into account.

My first two or three weeks were spent drawing out designs for a new range of bus and tram stops, which passed the time, but then things began to improve when thoughts of new tramcars began to stir in the upper echelons, and I became involved in much more interesting work. Looking back there did not then seem to be any firm idea as to just what form these were to take, so I began to produce side elevations and seating plans of what might be possible. One idea put forward by Mr Matterface was for a London tube-like arrangement with two double doors, and a lot of standing space but with a length restriction of around 42 ft and a maximum width of 7 ft 3 in. that proved to be impractical. Another suggestion was to follow the lines of the Feltham car then going into service in Leeds with a double door at the rear and a single width sliding exit door at the front, but here again capacity would be in the order of 22 seats, plus up to 12 standing on each platform as a maximum so that thought too was rejected, although it nearly came to be resurrected a year or two later.

Right: William (later Sir William) Chamberlain was the Oldham General Manager until 1925 when he moved to Leeds. At Leeds he sponsored the introduction of the fleet of 'Pivotal' tramcars. The first of these, No. 400, was built by Leeds City Tramways and had an Oldham look. The rest of the Leeds-built cars, plus 150 that came from contractors had a different front indicator layout that obstructed forward vision from upper deck seats.

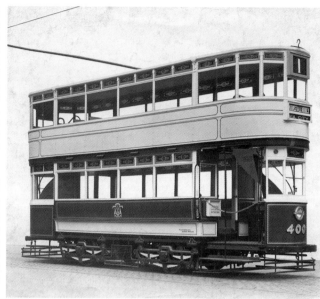

Below: The best trams in the Leeds fleet were the 104 'Horsefield' 'P35' cars, Nos. 151-254, that worked all over the system. Dating from 1930 they were good riding and thanks to upholstered seating throughout comfortable to travel on. This one is in the original livery, but in later years several different paint styles came to be applied.

Why we concentrated on single-deck trams I know not, perhaps Mr Findlay was the deciding factor here, but the earlier and forward looking subway plans seemed to be quite dead, and with the passenger loadings then being carried by the cars double-deckers would have appeared to be much more practical. But at no time did I have to run out any double-deck suggestions, instead I was told to go and look at the former Sunderland single-decker that was in the works, and see what could be done to bring it to completion.

As I said in my book *Looking at Buses* I went to Kirkstall works but did not see anything that looked like a single-deck tramcar, but then the body shop foreman Jonas Kay took me to the ruin for such it appeared to be. It is worth repeating that this Brush-bodied car of 1931 vintage arrived in Leeds in 1944 when it was painted grey and given a test run or two for here we were in the subway era. Then someone somewhere decided it was not quite the thing, so two fitters started work on the body, minus its maximum traction trucks, and cut off both end platforms this amputation also including the relevant roof sections. They then tackled the centre, taking out two complete bays, plus the attendant underframe, but now the main part of the tongue-and-grooved canvas-covered wooden roof was left *in situ*, so they performed this mighty piece of surgery with some delicacy. Why mighty? Well if I remember rightly the main underframe was of 8 in. by 5 in. channel, and to ensure this would never sag with old age, a substantial plate was bolted along it from end to end, and the wooden body frame then sat on top of the channel and was in turn secured to the plate. Remember too that all this cutting was done by hand. Once the cutting had been successfully accomplished a dropped frame section was put in place so the two halves were again joined up at ground level as it were and now presumably exhausted our two heroes retired and there the remains languished, gathering dust, and providing a home for various items of bodyshop junk, etc.

The first thing to do was to clear away the accumulation of years, and determine where we went from there. In view of all the work carried out there was little point in putting the centre back, so the centre entrance layout was confirmed. The end contours were determined by curved track clearance so the overall length came out at 41 ft 4 in. with the frame ends which were to carry the cabs following the lead set by the Felthams. A pair of ex-Liverpool heavy weight trucks of EMB manufacture were selected for use under No. 600, as the car came to be known, and so new crossmembers following the Liverpool 'Green Goddess' pattern were made up in the works, and fitted by the former surgical party, but then came a snag. The way in which the dropped centre had been made before the form of truck to be incorporated was known meant that, with Liverpool wheel sets, negotiating most of the system's corners would be virtually impossible, so two substantial packing pieces had to be fabricated to lift the whole underframe by a suitable amount. If you should go to Crich Tramway Museum and have the chance go under 600 and look at these feature for yourself. As it was a one-off curved glass for the front was not an option, so that part of the body resulted from having to work in flat glazing. I added the 'Lance Corporal' style moulding presuming this would continue the tradition set by cars Nos. 272, 273 and 274, thinking wrongly as it turned out that this was the way in which it would be finally painted.

The 'Middleton Bogies' were fine trams and gave a speedy ride through the woods on the private track to Middleton. The 16 in the production batch differed from No. 255, the prototype, which had offside staircases. All the others had their stairs on the nearside, i.e. on the left, as one gained the platform as this example clearly shows. No. 255 was new in June 1933.

By the end of the war Leeds badly needed some new trams. Consequently a prototype, No. 276, was turned out of Kirkstall works in 1948. Tenders had been invited for a production batch, but only one was forthcoming - from Roberts of Wakefield who built Sheffield's post-war cars and was prepared to supply the same design to Leeds. The Leeds management, however, wanted cars built to Leeds specification so No. 276 remained in solitary splendour. Despite a search in the office I could not find a single drawing of any part of No. 276, or even a general arrangement. I suspect it was built at Kirkstall works at the discretion of the staff there. Well done!

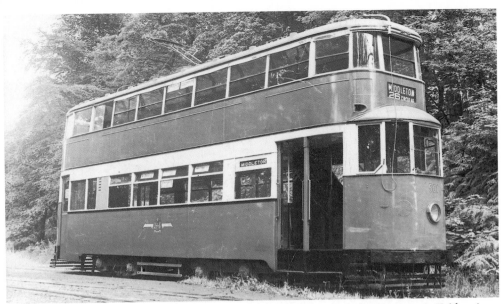

The need for new trams was partially filled by the acquisition of London Transport's 'Feltham' cars. Mr Matterface was the catalyst here coming to Leeds from London and having previously been with the Metropolitan Electric Tramways. The ex-MET cars with BTH equipment were quite reliable, but the former London United batch with GEC electrics were not so highly regarded, and not all came to enter service after purchase. This picture was taken of the first, No. 501, in Middleton woods, a route on which they did not work in my time in Leeds.

The carcass of car No. 600 was built by the Brush Company to the order of Sunderland Tramways. As No. 85 it went into service in March 1931 as a 50-seater. It was totally successful succeeding in saving the Villette Road route which, due to a low railway bridge, required single-deck trams. By January 1933 the bridge had been rebuilt to take double-deckers, No. 85 went into store in 1939 to be sold to Leeds in November 1944 for £375. This photograph was taken by Bob Parr and shows the car in Kirkstall works before rebuilding began.

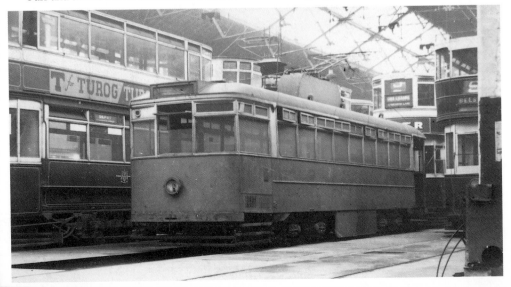

Right: Under construction an interior view of No. 600 showing the offset entrance to the saloon, the sliding windows, the parcel racks, grab rails and the recessed lighting fittings. Formica panels were fitted to the side casings. The front bulkhead was still in an uncompleted state.

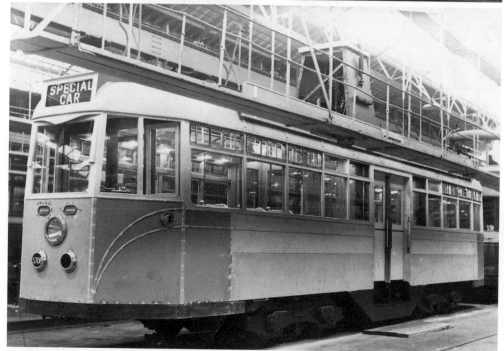

On 28th May, 1952 car No. 600 was close to completion. The frontal appearance was determined by the need to use flat glass. Electric equipment was in the roof-mounted tower, with the resistances partly hidden behind the advert boards with a centrally mounted destination blind. Despite it reaching this stage it had not entered service over a year later when I came to leave City Transport. It finally went into service on the Hunslet route in August 1954 where it continued until September 1957 when it was taken out of use.

Work then began on the interior, and the idea of having the entrances to each saloon offset, with access to locker space under the rear saloon transverse seats, then occurred and the pattern was set for the new production. By now it had been decided to order two basically similar new tramcars from Messrs C.H. Roe Ltd which were to incorporate the then most recent technology, one following the American 'PCC' 'Vambac' line of thought, the other being based on improved British traditional components. Here I have always felt that those in authority failed to push on with our local project, instead of concentrating on putting another Feltham or two on the road. We had all the material to hand to finish 600, and all the main drawings, for the handbrake gear, and the roof mounting of the electro-pneumatic control equipment had been finished.

As it was the rebuilding of 600 languished when it seemed obvious that if those in charge wanted to see the tramways continue then new rolling stock was going to be absolutely essential. The sooner the three single-deckers proved themselves, from both a traffic and engineering point of view, the sooner there would be the opportunity of seeing new and bulk orders placed. As it was the two car bodies were received from Roes, No. 602 first and a spell of double shift working took place. We started in the office at around ten in the morning and stayed until about three in the afternoon, then we returned, this time to Kirkstall works at about ten in the evening, did the necessary preparation work and when all was quiet went out to test the cars over all the routes until about three in the morning. Then it was off to bed to start again later in the morning.

Prior to all this we had paid a trip to Blackpool on a freezing cold day to ride on a 'Vambac' car or two there and learn what the local tramway engineers had to say about them. Comments of high current consumption were voiced but not the fault that became apparent one night early in the tests. No. 602 was being driven up the grade from Leeds Bridge to the Briggate junction and had to come to a stand before the traffic lights. When they turned to green the tram started to run backwards as there was a delay between the brake actuators (which put on the driveshaft drum brakes) coming off, and the control gear providing sufficient current to ensure forward motion, which in traffic could have been most embarrassing.

What was almost very embarrassing was the occasion when No. 602 was to be shown to the Press who were waiting our arrival in City Square. As we came along Wellington Street and were not all that many yards from our destination the power went off and we stopped. Victor Matterface then with considerable presence of mind leapt onto a following pivotal, pushed the driver to one side, came up behind 602 and gave it a considerable push so that it rolled gently into the square. As the pressman looked over this new marvel, frantic efforts were made, first to find the fault and then, as it was nothing very serious, to provide traction once more.

Another problem with 602 was due to the way in which the brake actuators came on. The motors were frame-mounted, and behind these secured to their casings were automobile-style drum brakes. These worked on the driveshafts again automobile-like, that ran to each of the axles, and so via bevel gears within the axle casings to the wheels. The brakes were operated by the Westinghouse actuators which came on when speed was reduced to approximately 8 mph. Unfortunately setting them so that they neither failed to come on properly nor overbraked and so produced a wheel skid was quite a problem so draughtsman or not, I came to spend some time under the car with a pressometer and other devices setting everything up as per book, only the adjustment never lasted long no matter how careful one was. Later we fitted more substantial actuator mounting brackets that improved the situation without totally curing the fault. I was fortunate in that nearly all the drawing office rolling stock work came my way, and some 90 per cent of this related to tramcars.

Bus work usually involved producing drawings to accompany new bus specifications, which were passed out to the manufacturers for tendering purposes, but then came the decision to buy some underfloor single-deck buses and here there was a question as to what body layout to adopt. Eventually orders were placed for three Leylands, three AECs and two Guys, all having centre entrance bodies, so following the tramway thought, but by the time they came into service I had left Swinegate for pastures new.

Other tramway work covered producing a scheme to reseat and update as far as was possible the retrucked pivotals that by now were running on Leeds-built Peckham 'P35' trucks, but fortunately in my view this came to be shelved Another unfulfilled plan was to convert at least some of the Felthams into single-deckers. In an endeavour to produce co-ordination in the engineering department Mr Parkinson had been promoted to the position of Chief Engineer, and was not over impressed by the way in which the Felthams consumed truck springs and, so it was said, did not do the rails joints much good due to their high axle loading. He therefore promoted what at first sight looked to be an easy conversion, when a new roof could be run from the existing cab roof lines, and the collector gear mounted thereon. I have the feeling that car No. 519 was chosen as the guinea pig, and the top deck panelling was soon removed but the steel framing beneath was a mass of rivets and fillets which needed to be carefully cut off manually if undue damage was not to result to the structure. After a few days it came to be appreciated that the end result would not justify all the labour and cost involved, and so one Feltham returned to traffic in its original two-deck state.

There was also the thought that in the interest of good engineering practice tramway car working tolerances should be much more like those to be found on buses so we looked at limits and fits on motor and axle bearings. This could well have been to the good if a production series of No. 602s had come into being, but such of course was never the case and so here was another endeavour that was quietly shelved.

It was around this time that I received another lesson in human behaviour. We worked three Saturday mornings out of four, then having a longer weekend. I came into the office after my long weekend on the Monday morning to be told that Mr Ellis wished to see me, so to his office I went, which was rather unusual as although he was my titular head I had had few occasions to have any direct contact with him. On entering his office he began to say how disappointed he was with me. He had it on good information that although saying at about 2.30 pm on Friday that I was going to Kirkstall works I had in fact not done so but had gone home. This was disgraceful! Consequently as I could not be trusted the privilege I had, being on a senior grade, of not having to clock on or off would be withdrawn forthwith so what had I to say for myself?

Now it so happened that I had gone to Kirkstall and had parked the family car by those of Mr Matterface and his works superintendent Mr Howell. We had stayed late discussing various problems until around 7.30 pm, or in other words about 2½ hours after normal finishing time. Then, being junior, I had waited whilst the gateman opened the exit doors, and then let my seniors precede me onto the main road.

Consequently I gently asked Mr Ellis if he would kindly ring Mr Matterface, and ask him an appropriate question. He gave me an odd look but did so, when the resulting conversation was very brief, and there followed a very profound apology when he made it quite plain as to where the source of his wrong information lay, without actually naming a name. This taught me two things. One remember the old school motto *Fide sed cui vide* or in other words 'Look in whom you trust' and two, when you have a position of authority inquire and then assess the evidence before pronouncing sentence.

The next spot of trouble to come my way was of a very different nature. Car No. 602 was delivered to Kirkstall on Monday 16th February, 1953, car No. 601 following on the 23rd March. Whilst it was being placed on its trucks and wired up the testing of No. 602 continued, but then on Wednesday 1st April No. 601 was ready for action and we sallied forth on its first test trip when all went well. One week later we took her out again in the small hours, but on returning to Kirkstall the tracks on which the single-deckers were usually parked were occupied so No. 601 was left on one further into the works that happened to be free.

Now not only were very few lights on in the works, but this track had on each side of it piles of steel tyre forgings, which meant there was little space between them and the car sides as the driver took it very slowly round the curve, a curve which did not seem to be used very frequently. There were only the two of us on the car as this movement took place, and we both heard a grinding noise as 601 was brought to a standstill. Then we went home, assuming the sound came from the dirty rails.

I returned to the office around 10.30 am when the door of our Chief Engineer's room which was right behind my desk was flung open and an angry Mr Parkinson bade me enter. In very few words I was commanded to go forth to Kirkstall works 'NOW', and after making inquiries come back and tell him what I had got wrong. The subject of my endeavour was to be car No. 601 but he did not enlighten me as to why my journey was to be so urgently necessary.

Off to KW I went to find that 601 was somewhat bent in four places where due to the radius of the curve the truck sides had swung over so far as to come through the body. Panic ensued!

Well we had supplied Roe's with information as to the radius of the sharpest curve on the system, or so we thought, but then guess what? This one was much sharper in curvature than any street tracks, and somehow that fact had never been noted, because nothing like 601 with its 41 ft 5¼ in. overall length, 16 ft 9 in. bogie centres, and 5 ft bogie wheelbase had ever been run onto it before.

Bob Parr was in City Square at the time No. 602 failed as it was about to be shown to the Press on 9th April, 1953. Although not obvious, No. 602 was being pushed by the 'Pivotal' behind with Mr Matterface at its controller. Believe me there was panic on board. I know, I was there!

To my mind, No. 601 with its EMB trucks and Metro-Vick equipment was the most practical of the pair of experimental single-deckers - put on the rails in 1953. So had a bulk order been forthcoming, 601 could well have formed the basis of the order. Bob Parr took this picture on 13th May after urgent repairs had been carried out to certain side panels.

Here No. 602 was different in that it had the wheels outside the truck frames so it could well have negotiated the track without problem. The easy way out was to ensure that the single-deckers were kept off this piece of trackwork. Authority came to be satisfied, and peace reigned once more.

The next excitement came on the 12th May when No. 602 received its inspection on behalf of the Ministry of Transport by Brigadier Langley. Our cold trip to Blackpool had resulted in one positive benefit as we were told that the Brigadier was hot on testing life guards. A dummy was required for the purpose, and no marks were to be gained if, when it was struck by the guard, the dummy burst and its innards, sawdust or straw, were scattered all over the track.

The hint was taken and a very substantial and quite lifelike dummy dressed in an old LCT uniform was loaded aboard No. 602 before we left for the test site which was on the reserved track between Belle Isle and Middleton. The tests were watched by numerous local inhabitants, including a mother and her small boy who were quite close to us as 'Fred' was unloaded and laid out on the track which was being kept clear of service cars. No. 602 was standing 300 yards or so away, and when the signal was given the driver put the control handle over, and the car started to speed up on its way to prove the efficacy or otherwise of the lifeguard.

At this point the little boy began to ask his mother what we were doing to 'that man', and as 602 came ever nearer his anguish rose proportionally. Thanks to Blackpool the test was a complete success, 'Fred' did not disintegrate, and the Brigadier was satisfied. But when we repeated the exercise with car No. 601 the following day one little boy was absent from the scene, so one can only hope he did not suffer from nightmares after going to bed.

Once Brigadier Langley had certified that the two cars were suitable for public use, driver training followed and then both went into service. No. 600 still remained in the works and work continued on it in a rather desultory fashion, to my regret as I wanted to see it finished, have a series of test rides on it, and discover just how it would perform but this was not to be.

Our Chief Engineer had told me, after saying I would not be involved with the buses, that he was proposing to send me to Kirkstall as assistant works superintendent, but this was not what I wanted even though it would have meant a form of promotion. As it was the whole single-deck tram effort was to be wasted. A change in political control at the Municipal elections as No. 601 was finishing its commissioning trials resulted in a tram scrapping party coming into power and it thus became obvious that in a few years there would be no trams and possibly no Kirkstall works. I had already had the experience of trying for a job elsewhere when on replying to a question as to what had I been working on the week of the interview with 'new trams', the Alderman concerned snorted, 'We scrapped those bloody things years ago' (actually in 1933).

I could see no future in Leeds City Transport and so I wrote to Leyland, Bristol and the Daimler Company asking if a suitable vacancy might exist. Each company replied and I was asked to attend for interview which I duly did, in the order Bristol, Leyland and Coventry.

The size of the Leyland drawing office quite put me off. Here I felt a junior could become lost, so sadly I rejected the thought of a move to Lancashire. The Bristol concern was much more interesting but the salary offered was much lower than the one I was enjoying at Leeds so economically Bristol was impossible, but what about Daimler's? Unfortunately on the day of my interview the Bus Engineer was away from work, but the chief car draughtsman told me only a few men worked on buses and he indicated that the pay would be above what I was then receiving at Swinegate, and so I accepted his offer. I put in my notice, receiving a nice letter back from Mr Findlay saying that he appreciated my reasons for going and felt that something would have to be done to ensure younger staff could become involved in bus work but this was all too late for me.

I should add here that not all my time had been spent on engineering matters. The undertaking was very short of staff so people from the offices were recruited to help out on various occasions when abnormal traffic levels could be expected. As a result I volunteered to try my hand at tramcar conducting. The first such occasion was on the day of the then very popular 'Childrens Days' when a whole range of appropriate activities took place on an annual basis in Roundhay Park, but sad to say I drew a very short straw . . . and so was the length of our railbound journeys. We left Swinegate Depot with a pivotal car (in original condition), stopped at Briggate to receive our instructions, and then spent a hectic afternoon running a shuttle service from Harehills to the Park Gates. We ran up the hill loaded to the hilt, and then back empty, to repeat the process. I lost count of just how many trips we made but taking in all the fares in the short time available kept me decidedly busy, whilst the iron shod staircase became ever steeper as the afternoon wore on. We had a short respite in the early evening and then spent our time until about 11 pm bringing the hordes back to the city centre. Fare levels then were very low by today's standards but at the end of a quite exhausting day I paid in well over £30 when cash in the bag exceeded apparent ticket sales. There was then an interesting sequel to all this on the Monday when 'fearsome' traffic superintendent J.B. Gill asked for the volunteers' waybills, looked them over, and proceeded to pass comment on a very select number, mine included.

My next excursion was very different. A firework display was to be held in the park so out we went with yet another 'Pivotal'. Sad to say it rained at the critical time so after about four trips from Briggate to the park I had sold 2s. 6d. worth of tickets but had only 2s. in the bag. I made good the deficiency out of my own money, and never did discover just where that 6d. loss arose.

By this time I had had some education in the art of tram driving. This resulted from the extension of my night-time testing stints when I started off on an open-fronted double-deck works car. We initially ran up and down Kirkstall Road, and as it was invariably raining I began to experience first-hand some of the conditions that Uncle George had told me about in earlier years. One was not travelling very fast but my, how wet one could become. As no vestibuled balcony cars then remained at Kirkstall I was not able to test out his complaint about their draught-making propensities.

As it was with Nos. 601 and 602 in service my workload greatly reduced, and so I was able to indulge in a spot of doodling. Looking back with the benefit of hindsight it is very apparent that our single-deck efforts were a lost cause right from the start. If these were to be the tramcars of the future then completion of all three cars should have been pushed on with as much urgency as possible. Once in service they should have been used to the maximum extent possible so as to prove their reliability or otherwise, and then as a result of the experience gained a bulk order could have been placed.

Had such a happy day ever arisen I suggest that car No. 601 would have formed the basis of that order for its was surely the most practical and reliable design. No. 602 was a very interesting technical endeavour, but as it then stood it was over complex, and certainly in my view required further development, but time for this was not really available in the conditions of 1953.

Loadings being what they were in that year it seemed to me that what Leeds really needed was some new four-wheeled double-decked cars to replace the ageing and obsolete pivotals or their 'P35'-trucked bretheren, so I had occupied my spare time drafting out a truckless version of such a vehicle. With a substantial underframe that would carry the two shaft drive motors, 602-style driving axles and EMB-style hornless truck suspension, a lighter weight 62/65 seater seemed to be very possible. Here again we are back with development time and cost, but if it had been given a lead a firm such as Metro-Cammell-Weymann with its bus and train production facilities could have produced a satisfactory product but it was never going to happen. As it was then, and still is, passengers who have paid a fare object to having to stand and so a 40 ft-plus long single-decker with only 34 seats would have been inadequate. But at least the single-deck programme had given me a great deal of very worthwhile experience and I had met with two of the great tramway names, namely Messrs Maley and Taunton, whilst working with Victor Matterface and his works superintendent Albert Howells, plus so many of the staff at Kirkstall, had been a most rewarding experience.

Now I was facing a very uncertain future. I had looked for years for a municipal transport opening, had finally found one, and now was giving it up of my own free will in the hope that I could develop my career in a rubber-tyred world. The steel wheels as they then existed in Leeds held out little hope for advancement, and I was much too young to accept the suggestion that I should take up the appointment at Kirkstall that had been offered.

In the expectation that someday I might make the grade I had come to the firm conclusion that membership of the Institute of Transport could be of advantage. I enrolled at the Leeds College of Commerce electing to pursue what should have been a four year course in just half that time, so during the weeks when the college was in session a night off became a decided luxury. Taking years one and two together really meant following instruction in six separate subjects, but I ignored the one that I felt I should be able to pass without further tuition. Fortunately for me the college timetable was such that the remaining five covered the five nights from Monday to Friday inclusive.

In view of what was to follow it was just as well that I made the effort! As I had some holiday due to me, my last day in the drawing office was on a Wednesday. That morning I left my most excellent Bramley lodgings and caught the 54 Rodley bus into the city for the last time. The sight of the now unused reserved tramway track to Bramley Town End and thence on the street to Half Mile Lane, made redundant only a week or two earlier, made me reflect that perhaps my decision to go was the right one in the circumstances. On reaching the office I packed up my belongings and made my farewells.

At this stage my chief draughtsman did not do a lot for my morale by detailing a list of men who over the years had left the office and who, with the exception of a gentleman who held office in another undertaking as head of the engineering department, had not done very well by any stretch of the imagination. He then added for good measure, 'Once someone has left they never ever come back', but here he was very wrong. Two decades later I was back, as his chief, when to my surprise he always addressed me as 'Sir' but to cover this part of the story we would need not two volumes but three, and no such production seems likely to see the light of day. But Volume Two, a rubber-tyred saga, certainly should, quite early in 2004.

Leeds had some pre-war AEC 'Regents' with robust Roe teak-framed bodies and some very dubious utility bodies on equally robust Daimler chassis so one bus job I had to tackle was to see if good bodies would fit on good chassis. The answer was in the affirmative and friend Bob Mack took this photograph of the end result.